www. comfortnsorrow . com

May God comfort you in this your time of loss

Living After DEATH

COMFORT FOR THOSE WHO MOURN

David C. McGee

WESTBOW°
PRESS
A DIVISION OF THOMAS NELSON
& ZONDERVAN

Scripture taken from the King James Version of the Bible.

Scripture quotations cited as MSG are from *THE MESSAGE*. Copyright
© by Eugene H. Peterson 1993, 1994, 1995, 1996, 2000, 2001,
2002. Used by permission of NavPress Publishing Group.

WestBow Press books may be ordered through booksellers or by contacting:

WestBow Press
A Division of Thomas Nelson & Zondervan
1663 Liberty Drive
Bloomington, IN 47403
www.westbowpress.com
1 (866) 928-1240

Because of the dynamic nature of the Internet, any web addresses or
links contained in this book may have changed since publication and may
no longer be valid. The views expressed in this work are solely those
of the author and do not necessarily reflect the views of the publisher,
and the publisher hereby disclaims any responsibility for them.

Any people depicted in stock imagery provided by Thinkstock are models,
and such images are being used for illustrative purposes only.
Certain stock imagery © Thinkstock.

ISBN: 978-1-4908-8297-0 (sc)
ISBN: 978-1-4908-8298-7 (hc)
ISBN: 978-1-4908-8296-3 (e)

Library of Congress Control Number: 2015908826

Print information available on the last page.

WestBow Press rev. date: 6/25/2015

Contents

The saddest thing in life would be to live and
die and no one grieve your loss.

I. Section One

I Cannot Believe this has Happened

Unit 1

Grief Introduction

The obvious is that every life will experience the death of a loved one or the death of a person of close personal relationship. The not so obvious is how we will respond mentally, emotionally, physically, and spiritually. What effect will faith have on this sorrow, this grief? The pain of death will touch every life; it cannot be avoided. No one and no family is exempt. It is certain that life experiences loss, and with loss comes grief. Grieving is our response to this lost connection, often centering on death, but grief will be connected to any important wound to life. (Any loss to life that is valued can create grief, such as the loss of a job, divorce, unfulfilled dreams, moving, illness, stroke, etc.)

Your grief reaction is as unique and individualistic as you are, as unique as the relationship lost, and as distinctive as the anticipated life after injury. Each individual has his or her own expressions of love, and you will have your own expression of loss. This special makeup will lead each individual into and through his or her peculiar grief response. The distinctiveness of personal grief arises from one's values, culture, family, community, spiritual beliefs, and understanding of loss and of death. No two people will grieve the same, but there are similarities. As individuals, we can complicate the grief experience by a lack of understanding concerning grief and how loss interacts with our present lives. Knowledge does not cancel out grief, but it helps in understanding and expressing the changing features that each person displays in grieving. Knowledge is an anchor to the grieving process. But although an anchor holds a ship, it does not calm the troubled sea.

Grieving presents challenges to everyday living beginning the moment someone informs you of a death. Each day will have its own uniqueness. The memories, the absence of your loved one, and that day's activities merge into a day that can feel like a blender. And as soon as things begin to settle, something or someone comes along, pushes the start button, and life is again in a spin.

The following information and stories illustrate the grieving process, bringing to you information and experiences that accompany grief. Many carry the idea that there is something wrong with them when this grief steals its way into life because they have never experienced it before—or at least not to this extent. The bereaved question whether they can survive for another hour or another day. Grief is intense and will express itself, but you are not alone on this path of grief. Every individual has traveled or will travel this path.

The importance of having someone explain grief and the distinctive responses we will have to it will not take away the grieving experience; however, it will become an anchor in knowing that you are not "crazy." This is normal, and there are others like you. Disclosing grief by relating the experience of loss through conversations, feelings, descriptions, information, and inquiries can help in lessening the pressure associated with thinking that personal grief is abnormal or simply a mistake. Many consider the route of grief to be the most difficult course ever experienced.

Unit 2

Goal

The goal for our time together is to deal with that which has taken place in a healing way, discovering and dealing with the "new now" and knowing there is a future. Handling grief is not as simple as giving things away or being so busy that we have no time to think. Grieving is not a single act but a series of things accomplished over a period of time—sometimes years. Do not be frightened by the reference to *years*. Focus on accomplishing today's task, and the period of time needed will take care of itself. In the beginning, grief can be overwhelming; for some individuals, it will include inactivity with no strength or desire to get through the next hour. Others are consumed with busyness: an endless motion pushing the self to the limits so as not to allow unwanted thoughts to enter. In handling or dealing with grief, you must have openness to each area of life, face these volatile places with assurance knowing that you have survived the event, and know that you can deal with the memory. This will take time, and as you will notice being identified several times over, there is no rush or push to an imagined finish. We approach today with its valued thoughts and experiences, and we seek to deal with them in manageable segments.

The grieving experience is not only for those surviving the death of a loved one but also encompasses all who have experienced any significant loss in life. The support offered in the stories and thoughts originates from a desire to help those experiencing a shattering loss—primarily those grieving the death of a loved one. The information, stories, and illustrations are derived from many years' experience serving as a pastor, counselor, chaplain, hospice chaplain, and bereavement facilitator.

One other thought as we begin to work through these pages: Grief can be categorized in many ways, such as seasons, stages, phases, timelines, and periods. These classifications are helpful, and grief does fall into these spaces. However, in the pages that follow, grieving is presented as being very fluid and shifting, as something moving forward and backward—and something that even gets stuck at times. The transference presented here focuses not so much on finding a place to measure where one's grief is, but rather on being open and honest with ourselves, with our relationships (both past and present), and with feelings, thoughts, and emotions as they now present themselves.

Being open to the "now" means being open to what is presenting itself today. By dealing with these presentations in manageable segments, we find ourselves moving through the grief experience at a personal pace established by our relationships and our physical, spiritual, emotional, and mental makeup. Locating the range of grief for one's life is as simple as asking, Where am I now? Your grief is not to be found in comparing yourself to another's—this is simply not fair to you or the other person. Comparisons will be determined by the day. One day it will be your strengths compared to the person's weakness, and you will feel strong. When you feel weak, the comparison will be their strength to your weakness, making matters worse. Everyone will grieve differently. Personal awareness involves answering questions such as, Where was I yesterday, and what has changed? Am I avoiding, or am I pushing? Am I willfully avoiding leaving the present? Or am I dealing with life events as they arise each day? Deal with today and it will have a meaningful effect on what happens tomorrow. This change is something we do not desire. Now, since death has transformed life forever, we are very guarded about what we willfully want to alter. For now, life is difficult, for sometimes the moments feel like they will never end. You may think, *I want to wake from this nightmare and find myself normal again.* There is no rush, nor is there a push. This is dealing with grief as presented, trying to get through this moment.

Unit 3

Empathy and Direction

There are those in grief who resist help from others because they view support as pity. But there is a difference between pity and empathy. Pity is saying, "Oh, you poor thing." Empathy is more of a two-layered approach to "being moved" by another's loss, but accompanying this "being moved" is a consideration of the question, "How can I help?" It is impossible to know the details of each life situation or each personality, but allow the offer of support and empathy to at least be something you consider.

Very few life experiences can ever compare with the death of a loved one. As you continue to read these pages, you will find many thoughts and illustrations. Some of these will neatly fit into your life, while others will appear to be out of sync. If you have ever lived in a geographic area that experiences the four seasons, you are well aware that when it is ten degrees below zero, you do not go outside wearing only your swimming trunks, and when it is ninety-eight degrees, you do not pull out the down winter coat to take a walk. Likewise, with grief spanning numerous seasons, there are ideas and actions that are appropriate and helpful in one season of grief that will not be appropriate or work in another (e.g., a winter coat on a summer day). There will be thoughts presented that make little sense for what you experience today. Save the winter coat for winter. Perhaps someday the thought will be appropriate for that season. Give yourself permission to be in the grief season of what has happened and what is currently happening in your life.

The reasoning for not trying to place oneself or discover whether one is halfway through grief or three quarters of the way finished with grief can be illustrated by imagining a map of the United States before us. New York City is where we start, and San Diego, California, is the destination. If we were to plan to drive from New York City to San Diego, reason asserts that we pick the most direct route, use the best roads, push hard, drive at night, cover a large number of miles per day, and try to arrive sooner than we would if we simply drove six hours a day. With this perception of start and finish, the attention focuses on time, how far we have come, and how far we have to travel. We like the order of miles, days, and lengths of time as a way to calculate just how long this trip will take.

Grief is not like a calculated drive from coast to coast. It is not like driving one hundred miles and then resting, driving another one hundred miles and resting again, and stopping for the night to begin again in the morning. Grief is more like traveling from New York City to San Diego by stopping first in Miami and then going back up to Atlanta, over to Houston, up to Chicago, back to Cleveland, out to St. Louis, and then finding ourselves back where we started in New York City. We feel like this can't be normal. We question, Where in the world am I going, and when will I get to San Diego? Of course, there will be unscheduled stops along the way.

Real life situations can mirror the grief journey, once while traveling, a family stopped at a rest area on Interstate 70 going west through the state of Indiana. They spread the map of the United States on the hood of the car and asked, "Which way is New York City?" They located their position on the map and found that they needed to be on the eastbound side of the interstate instead of the westbound. The family had been traveling for several hours in the wrong direction. With grief, information and the freedom to express emotions let us know we are headed in the right direction even if we go to Miami on our way to San Diego. So if you are wondering, *How long can this grief journey take?* there are many variables in grieving, but grief is not about time or distance traveled. It is about openness and the desire to deal with whatever comes in life, past, present or future, knowing the direction you need to travel, and stopping often. We need to recognize that each stop, each memory, and each emotion has an attached value; we need to take a break and stay for a time.

When traveling to a destination, the focus is on getting there, not on the journey. Grief, however, is about the day-to-day journey. Just as this grief journey is not what we expect, so the destination will not be where we think it should end. Must we have goals and a destination in mind? Yes, but along the way, these may change. When our family traveled, it was within a period of one week or, at the most, a two-week vacation. The goal was to get to the destination and start the vacation. We needed to be there at check-in to unpack; we had the room for six days. Our trips were about destinations, about getting there and back home just before going to work. There was no stopping. We needed to get where we were going.

In grief, the destination is not clear, so planning a trip will require some help. We really do not know where this will end up, but ready or not, the grief journey has begun. Perhaps you have heard the saying, "It's not about the destination; it's about the journey." That is very appropriate for grieving. The journey to the "new normal" is about being yourself right where you are and being open with thoughts, feelings, memories, today's activity, and tomorrows' dreams. In grieving, as soon as you think you have a direction or a destination in mind, something cuts in, the road is closed, there's a detour, or you get a "can't get there from here" feeling. Be patient, and be kind to yourself. There's no rush or push. Take a deep breath, and let us take a ride together, perhaps just have a conversation together. We will travel this laid-back road knowing there will be a time when we reach our goal, but not today.

Unit 4

You're Story

Every person has a story, a very important story of life and life events that brought him or her to this place in time, a place of experiencing sorrow, loss, and grief. Every life story is significant, especially where love has placed added value to a particular relationship. If we were sitting together, I would ask you to tell me your story. Begin with how this life, this dream, began for you, not at the time of the tragedy or the hardship but at the beginning, when the story first got underway, where love, hope, and relationship come together. Tell about the opening, when you encountered the person who became interwoven into the fabric of your life. I think of retelling the story as checking into the details to guarantee they are still all secure. We are confirming life events woven together.

Grief is not about undoing a life, untying the years, or unweaving days from one another. Grieving is distinguishing when that final stitch was made together, recognizing that one life lives on and one does not. Forced separation happened, and death came and, as one person stated, "stole my loved one." This is the pain of death, when the stitching of life changed, where two lives stopped and now there is one. This is a challenging, demanding place where change came by force, mandating that your life would change forever. Take time to remember; write your thoughts in a journal.

Unit 5

Am I Normal?

One question that often arises is, "Am I normal?" When we pause to consider it, the normal grief experience is abnormal to everyday life before the death of a loved one. This change (from life before the death to life now, in which grief is experienced) is the main reason so many question themselves about how they are presently living.

Similarly, relational questions come forward: "Did they know I loved them?" Self-doubt arises, as if the presence of grief is a signal that a person did something wrong or something was left out. Perhaps in a time of frustration or fatigue, something said or thought now haunts the grieving. Questioning ourselves is a normal part of review; it is okay to review and ask questions as long as you answer the questions thoroughly and in the context of the moment. Remember, some people are verbal in their expressions of love, while some are quiet. The key is that, for many, everyday interactions went by without their stating what these people meant to them. There is not a relationship in which the bereaved couldn't stand to have been more expressive, but the relationship often takes on the character of things understood but not said. This would be "things" that were simply understood or designated as unspoken. There are expressions we wish we had said or done, but we always thought there would be time. We were waiting until the time was right to bring up the subject or simply convey the assurance that we love them. People of both types of personalities—the verbal and the not-so-verbal—will ask the same question: "Do you think they knew I loved them?" Many questions find their answers in the relationship shared, the personality of each, and the perception of the bereaved, the "understood" things not often spoken.

As we pause for a moment, we look at the thought behind the statements, "If I did not love them so much, I would not hurt so severely," or "If I had told them how much I love them, I would not hurt so intensely." Some people search for reasons they hurt so deeply, as if there has to be a reason that death causes so much pain. It is the intense pain of loss that causes the hurt, not necessarily a statement left unsaid. When you love, whether you have an expressive personality, if you are one who speaks what you think or feel, or if you are one not expressive, where you like to keep things within and speak only when it is necessary, death hurts. Questions arise in the replay of events and things said or left unsaid. Guilt feelings arise.

There were times in group sessions when I would respond in jest when someone would ask the question, "Am I normal?" I expressed that we would work to help them get back to "their normal, abnormal self." It was a way to reframe the question while injecting a little humor when considering what is "normal." What did his or her prior normal self look like, the self before death, before loss came? Grief expression is normal when we experience loss, but grief expression is abnormal to everyday life that has not experienced loss. This is the reason grief feels so out of place, so foreign to what was the normal everyday life.

Think of what happens while grieving the death of a loved one. If the bereaved conducted their lives before death as they do in grief, would this be normal? No. Death changes how we view life and loss and how we live each day, especially in the first months. I think of the adult son coming home from work and seeing his deceased mother standing at the window waiting for him to get home. This is the location his mother always stood waiting for him to arrive before she put supper on the table. Seeing a deceased loved one in a familiar place, or dreaming of the deceased and hoping the dream will not end, happens. These dreams are not like any other; they are so real that we believe the loved one is there in the room or are certain we saw the deceased walking in a store, heard their voice call your name. In grief, these are shared experiences, but to have these experiences prior to a death experience would be reason to question one's mental health. The impulsive searching for someone who has died wanting to say good-bye, to hold him or her one more time, to hear his or her voice again bring on unusual feelings. These thoughts or desires never existed before your loved one died. These experiences cause the bereaved to question their normalcy. So is this normal? Yes.

A helpful thought, but one that is obvious, is that it will take one year to go through many of the firsts. No matter how hard we push, it will take one full year to have most of the first-time experiences. Sometimes we overlook the apparent, but regardless of how hard you push toward the future or how hard you want to stay in the past and not let go, each day will come and go, and in time, a year will have passed and the one-year anniversary will come. One year, then two years, then five years—grieving is not about time; it is about dealing, talking, feeling, and doing the daily activities that present themselves. We sort through and complete this first year not all at once but in manageable segments. If time were the healer of all wounds, then putting in time would be the answer. It would be like a birthday—it comes each year, so we would just need to put in the time and wait. But grieving is not about putting in time but about focusing on the effort of dealing, talking, feeling, and doing. Grief is not running from sorrow but being drawn toward it and facing the loss as it is daily presented.

Guides in grief are not a set of constraints or a set of years, months, or days for achievement of a grief assignment. Nor are they simply identifying difficulties and looking to the passage of time as a marker to identify how "well" one grieves. These fail to accomplish the goal of healing the wounded heart. We learn to live without someone's physical presence, learn to live with the loss. The negative concept of time or using time as a rule for grieving and applying pressure is often done if someone needs years to move through his or her grief. Does that make that person "worse" than anyone else or indicate that he or she "loved more deeply" than someone else who may have accomplished his or her grief in a shorter period? The variables in grieving are endless. No two persons are alike, and no two relationships are alike. Beyond that, people's grief is affected by different cultures, different backgrounds, their support structures, what has happened, how it happened, to whom it happened, the years together, the years expected to be together, and so on. All this and much more make up the response to loss, to death, to grieving.

A dominant difficulty that presents itself is, "Grief is not what I thought it would be." What we imagine this loss response would be is far from what it is, and what is happening is much different from what was expected. However, when grief is nothing like imagined, we perceive that something is wrong with how we are grieving. Not so—this is the normal world of grief. However, do not dismiss the opportunity to seek professional help in working through this process. The reality of grief is far different than anticipated, so be kind to yourself as you move through this process.

Take a deep breath and pause; we are not in a hurry. We will walk through these thoughts together. The goal is to work through the difficult moments, the difficult daily moments, and then through the difficult days. We will work through everything that presents itself as a struggle to expose the heartache with love and understanding until we have more good moments than bad. No rush, no push in uncovering what has happened and what is happening, doing so in manageable segments. We do not run from the experience; we move toward it by allowing each moment to bring its memory or feeling, and often we may not know what to do with this experience but deal as best we can.

Each moment can become a piece of a puzzle that we lay upon a table, sorting, placing pieces together as part of a larger, developing picture. The importance of each piece is discussed, its value to the picture declared, or perhaps we are not aware of its value until it is placed. Have you ever put a puzzle together and found pieces that looked like they belonged to another puzzle? Some of today's empty spaces are completed with tomorrow's experiences. Some of the missing pieces are keys to understanding the picture before us, and we do not have those pieces yet. No rush, no push— in time and with effort, grief necessitates the puzzle's coming together. Daily, grief feels the same, but the days are not the same; each day has its own distinctive shape. Allow yourself to make the pieces as you go, and later the picture will come into focus. With puzzles, some pieces have shapes so similar that it is hard to tell them apart. So it appears with daily grief. Although we think each day is the same as the day before, it is not. Possibly, at first, there are only minute changes, but as life continues, some days will have very distinct fluctuations in shape. Some images will need to be discussed, handled, cried over, laughed with, and set aside until we know in what way these will add to the completion of the picture. Grief, as ordinary life before grief, has the expression of all emotion. For this reason, grief needs to be a shared experience, even as love is a shared experience. Allow yourself to speak with family, friends, someone who listens well and, where possible, allow them to walk with you, hearing your story and for you to hear theirs. Remember, attached to each piece of the puzzle is a story.

Unit 6

I Can Do This Myself

We unfairly tell ourselves, *I can handle this alone, This loss is no different than other losses in life*, which were "toughed out," *Keep a stiff upper lip, nose to the grindstone, shoulder to the wheel. I can do this myself.* Grief is not about making the journey alone, nor is it about toughing it out. It's not about denial of feelings or pushing on through the difficult times as if nothing happened. Grief is not about being so busy that you have no time to think.

One person called my office and wanted help. He had been reading a book about grief and decided he had arrived at an impasse; he was stuck in this grief process and only needed to resolve one problem to finish his grief. I am sure the author of the book did not intend the reader to approach the information as a calculated work assignment so that, when completed, the participant graduates from grief to move on with his life. The individual asking the question thought this problem was preventing him from accomplishing, finishing his grief over the death of his spouse. He mentioned that it had been only six months since his spouse had died, and his goal to be "normal" lie at the conclusion of this chapter. This is like reading a driver's manual and assuming you know how to drive. These misunderstandings happen in any area of life where the goal is an imagined finish line that needs to be reached. The wrong conclusion of grief is thinking one can arrive at some place and never think of the deceased loved one again. This will never happen, and this is not the goal. We can hope that there is somewhere in the future where the impact of death and this loss are no longer the dominant thoughts.

One of my friends in health care spoke of knowing what the books on grief say; she has helped many terminally ill patients with their physical needs and supported families in their immediate grief. It took the death of her own loved one to bring this grief reality to her understanding, to know what this sorrow demands. "I never knew it would be like this," she said. Knowing what the books say but having never had the impact of personal loss is a difficult place to be; the realities are different from what was expected after reading a textbook. The objective for these pages is to present information and experiences in a way that you may receive the information and intertwine it with your personal experience. The information presented is to help in anchoring life in this unsettled time. The anchor holds the ship in place, but the anchor does not calm the troubled sea.

Unit 7

No Instant Formula

There is no formula to bring instant healing to a grieving heart. There are ideas, words of comfort, and physical support that help hold one in the moment—anchors. With the comfort comes a hope that we will make it through to the next moment. Another question that arises is, "At times I find an ease from grief, a time of peace, but the pain returns. Was the ease only a fluke? Am I never getting beyond this?" The feeling of a moment's peace does not indicate that we have arrived at the end of the grieving process. Each step, each question asked, each relived moment, each answer, and each moment of peace are all part of the rebuilding process, the laying of a footing for the next move. There will be many such experiences; each is important in its own way.

Grief is not what you thought it would be. Grief often is not what others tell you it is. Grief has come upon your life in ways not perceived, and now with its full impact, there is a want for something to hold onto, some truths that will help in making it through today. Grieving is difficult enough without the added self-pressure of thoughts like, *I have gone nuts, I must be crazy because I cry all the time*, *I don't want to go out*, *I don't want to go home*, and *When I do go out I don't want to see anyone.* Some people have told me things like, "I shop in a neighboring town where no one knows me so I do not have to answer that question, 'How are you doing?'" Another said, "I shop at night. I never used to shop at night. I want to avoid people. I know at night no one will talk to me." Finally, one person told me, "I can't sleep, so I go shopping at three in the morning." When I asked this individual what she bought at three in the morning, she replied, "I buy a jar of peanut butter, and I have over fifty jars." Each one grieves differently. Each one does his or her own particular thing. The person who had fifty jars of peanut butter eventually donated them to a food bank and started sleeping all night, but it took time and was a struggle. For her, the struggle was that she was afraid to dream. Remember, grief is something understood only as it is experienced. Like driving a car, you can read and understand all the mechanics of an engine, know all the rules of the road, and be familiar with every button on the dash, but the experience of driving will be completely different from reading a manual. Driving a small car is different than driving an SUV, and driving a sports car is different still. And then driving a tractor-trailer—you understand the picture. All are driving, but each vehicle is different; they are not the same. Once you have driven, then the information begins to make sense; it begins to fit into the driving experience. You are in the grief experience. It is important to read and understand as much as possible. The material read may apply to your life, and it may not. You are an individual, your relationship was unique, and your grief will be distinctively yours.

Unit 8

Until Death Do Us Part

The covenant in marriage is "until death do us part." The covenant is complete, but the desire to continue the relationship is still there. Our loving relationships in which we invest ourselves in others and they in us—these important life attachments—feel like they will go on forever, but abruptly, they have ended. "Will I ever be happy again?" The answer is yes, but happiness is based on happenings. Joy is that which resides in the heart. When a spouse dies, there are many areas to be worked through and, in many cases, the list is overwhelming. Remember, in any relationship, there are two individuals learning to live as one. There were the duties that one was better at than the other. When one dies, all of his or her duties now fall upon the survivor. There is a reason we gave the duties away. We never liked them or never wanted to learn. Now we have to learn how these things are done. One widow explained, "I get angry at him. He always put gas in the car. Now fifty-four years later I am pulling into a gas station and have no idea where the gas tank is located." Life is learning to live with, and now without, someone.

Unit 9

Hitting Bottom

Grief is multidirectional; it is this pulling backward to the past and pushing forward to the future, downward in our emotions and upward in faith. We are constantly fluctuating somewhere amid the four. Early in the grieving process, we spend a lot of time in the past while trying to adjust to the present. Further along, we spend more time thinking of the future than the past and adjusting to the present. Sometime in the early weeks or months of grief comes the awareness of life gradually flowing in a downward direction, when people often say, "I feel like this is getting worse." No matter what is done, life is not as good as we think it should be; in fact, it feels worse than the day before. The loss reality becomes greater. We wonder if there is something wrong with us. Will there be a bottom? The answer is yes—there will be a bottom to the grief experience, and it was not at the time of the death or in the days after the funeral. The bottom comes at some point in those months, or longer, following death, when we realize that our loved ones are not coming home. One of the hardest moments in the grief experience is when we come face to face with this reality: "They are not coming back."

Personally, one of my most difficult times in helping others was in speaking with a mother whose daughter had died in a car accident. The daughter was sixteen. We spent many counseling hours together speaking of the loss, reviewing and remembering. Then one day, she looked at me and said, "You mean my little girl is not coming home?" This realization came eighteen months after the accident. Everyone is different. Some come to this realization in a few months; for some it takes longer. What goes into this realization is dependent on the relationship, our personal makeup, how they died, what difficulties need to be worked through, our understanding of death, and numerous other things. The length of time is not a reflection of strength, weakness, better or worse, good or bad. The focus is the grieving individual, not deflecting grief as if avoidance were the goal.

Focus is allowing you to be open, to be drawn to the memory or feeling by giving expression in a healing way (speaking, keeping a journal, thinking, praying, remembering). This is the life you lived with the one you love. Remembering is not a bad thing. Grieving their absence is our way of healing. We do so in manageable segments.

Unit 10

Trauma: Deep Emotional Wound

The present trauma that has you reading this may not appear to be like any other loss experiences, but you have been here before—not to this emotional depth, but you have been through loss before. You have survived many varied changes, many different losses in your life. The difference between now and then is the relationship, the increased emotional bond that is attached to the present loss. This intense amplification of emotions makes one feel out of control. Pause and think of the emotions experienced in this time of grief and sorrow. If you were to list the emotions that are bombarding you, what would they be? They are the same emotional responses as you have had on other occasions, but at this time, the intensity is much greater. This is what makes these emotions feel different and leave the impression of being out of control. Take a few minutes to write down all of the emotions and feelings that you have right now. After you have written them down, come back to this place.

The emotions, feelings, and thoughts you have listed are similar to those you have experienced in the past, but they are on an entirely different level. The impression given by grief is different because of the intensity of how the emotions, feelings, and thoughts manifest themselves. They are at a level they have never been before. You may wonder, *If I have experienced these same things before, why do they feel so different?* Grief is intense and will appear different from what was experienced before. This is partly why many feel that grieving makes them out of control. The goal here is to recognize that the emotions and feelings are not strangers; they have been with you all of your life. Now in the present grief, there is a frustration, a fear of feeling a loss of control, a determined avoidance of remembering the past by swallowing hard and changing thoughts. At this time, the tears come, and there is no stopping them. The present event that is beyond our emotional control, beyond our ability to change, brings a feeling of helplessness that nothing can make the loss different, that nothing can alter what has happened. There is no one thing that will suddenly take grief away. The grief journey will take time. For this time, now, know that what you have written in your journal is important to you. Grief is a normal response to an abnormal situation—loss, death, and change. It will be good again, just not today. Perhaps take some time with your thoughts and again write them down, making clear what you are thinking, missing, and feeling in your journal. Express your understanding of what has happened and what is happening.

Unit 11

Tears

Some people question, "If I allow myself to cry, it will not stop. My tears are overwhelming. Will I be able to stop crying?" Yes, the tears will stop, perhaps in five minutes, an hour, or a few days, but they will stop. If this is what you need, then allow this expression. The fear of allowing oneself to start crying is real; we worry that if we begin crying, we will be out of control. The death experienced now may be greater than any previous loss; that is why the tears and other expressions make us feel we are out of control. This fear of allowing tears creates an anxiousness that only intensifies the grieving experience, the fear of tears. "Is the amount of time I cry good or bad?" others ask. Some say they have cried until they cannot cry anymore and then start crying again. If the moment and the memory find expression in tears, allow them to flow.

There are places where tears are considered unacceptable, such as at work or in social or public gatherings, because others are uncomfortable with such expressions. Grieving will occur in many different places, some where the two of you were together and some in places you wish he or she was there to experience. Often, the workplace offers a quieter, less expressive grief experience because, typically, the deceased was not part of that everyday life. If you are at a social gathering, the tears come, and you become aware that they are not going to stop, excuse yourself, thank the host, assure him or her that all is okay, and return home. It is better to venture out and need to return home than to stay in the house afraid to leave. The next outing, frequently, is a little easier, but even if it is not, getting out is important.

Often, individuals who construct emotional barriers to block their grief expression end up prolonging the grieving process to the point that these barriers become prisons. When these obstructions are in place, a lot of energy is exerted keeping the wall secure and limiting access to any stimulus that could stir the memories. The fear of being out of emotional control is often worse than simply allowing oneself to cry. That fear comes from not wanting to appear weak or to be embarrassed in front of others or perceived as out of control, as if you are "losing it." If you need to leave a certain place, then leave and go back later. Emotional responses and the struggle you experience will change with time, but there must be a first time. Dismantling fears occurs as we face them, deal with them, and speak of what makes them so dreaded. We do not need to create fears or generate something to cry over, nor should we deny the impact of a loved one's death. The grief response is an expression of sorrow, which is as normal as loving.

Unit 12

Emotions

*E*motion is defined as "a: the affective aspect of consciousness: feeling; b: a state of feeling; c:a conscious mental reaction (as anger or fear) subjectively experienced as strong feeling usually directed toward a specific object and typically accompanied by physiological and behavioral changes in the body" (2014 Merriam-Webster's Dictionary). The thing about emotions is that while we all have them and all express them, many just do not understand them. Some state of their emotions, "They just get in the way."

I smile in wonder with those who declare, "I have my emotions under control." Controlling the emotions is not the problem; it is finding an appropriate way to express them. To those who have "never emotionally lost control," I question what that statement looks like in real life. Perhaps such a person throws a chair across the room in anger and then later state that he has always maintained control of his emotions because he has never shed a tear. With the man who stated that he and his wife "never had an argument," the rest of the story from her perspective was, "He beat me when I did not do what he wanted." Even so, she believed it was her fault; she felt penitent because she made him angry. In death, many of the past incidents involved in the relationship surface. Some people are glad the deceased person can no longer torment them. There is relief. "It was torment living with them," they may say. "Now I feel so guilty for having such thoughts." Death, for some, is a release from the prison of commitment that they shared with the departed. "There were very few happy moments that we shared together," I have heard people say. "Of the twenty years together, we had two good years."

The other extreme is those who feel guilty for not getting a glass of water in the middle of the night because they were so tired that they did not hear the loved one's request. One person spoke of her guilt over going to get groceries and leaving the loved one alone for an hour. Guilt can torment the survivors who arrived at the decision that it was okay for their loved ones to die because their pain and suffering would be over. "I wish I had never said that," they might say. Guilt needs only a moment to destroy a lifetime of caring. You could have a hundred years of good and thirty seconds of perceived failure, and guilt will use the thirty seconds to destroy the hundred years. Guilt is a topic we will discuss later, but we see the manipulative behavior it creates. Guilt, here, is an abusive manipulator.

Unit 13

Love

Recognize that there are different levels of love that produce different levels of loss. You may love your car, love your house, love the weather, love your pet, love your job, love your friends, love your child, love your spouse, love your parents, and love your siblings. All are love relationships, but not all occupy the same place of emotional attachment or stir the same commitment. Not all have the same relational value. Loss comes in many forms as well; there's the sadness that it rained on your outdoor wedding, it rained on your picnic, rain cancelled a ballgame—a World Series to which you had tickets. The experiences of hitting a pole with your new car, canceling a prepaid trip with no refund, and moving all involve loss, but the individual experiencing the loss determines the value. Each loss will bring its own level of grief or sadness based on the relationship or expectation. Your child's team losing in the playoffs and your child dying are two extremely different losses. Perhaps your best friend moved away during childhood, or you moved as an adult because of work—many life experiences have points of grief. Managing losses that are of lesser emotional value sets a pattern or establishes similarities in how one deals with major losses. The major loss is immensely more intense. Major losses such as the death of a spouse, the death of a child, a severe stroke, and divorce are much greater on the personal, relational level. No amount of preparation can equip someone for these events. Even if a loved one has been ill for a long period of time, death is still a shock. "I told them many times in the last week that it was all right for them to go, but I never thought their death would hit me like this," one person said.

I recall an individual who spoke with me concerning his thoughts on my grief experience; he said, "I would have it easy if someone close to me died because I know all about grief." His reasoning came from a factual, intellectual approach. He surmised that if someone understands the process, he or she would not have to emotionally go through the process, as if knowledge would be the key to bypassing the emotional response to death. Knowledge helps us *understand* the path through grief but does not stop one from walking the path. Knowledge helps in understanding the road, the direction we are going, and the path we are traveling, but in no way is it able to cancel traveling the path through the grief experience.

We may possess the map, but unless we get in the car and travel the road, we will never reach the destination. If you sit in your car and turn the steering wheel all while staying in the driveway, nothing really changes. However, if you start the engine, place the car in drive, apply the gas, and steer yourself out onto the road, and turning the wheel as you are in motion affects the direction the car will go. Knowledge of grief is the road map that informs us as to the direction we are going and exactly where we are presently located. The map can identify the many roads we can travel. Nevertheless, as we will discover, planning a route is good, but there will be many changes made along the way. The one good thing is that we have a map of the region so that no matter where we travel, we are not lost. We are not off the map.

When I traveled to Israel a number of years ago, I remember thinking, *No matter how I try, I cannot walk home or drive home from here.* This was a first for me. It was a different feeling, one I had never experienced before. Grieving can produce a similar feeling: No matter how hard we try, we cannot get back to yesterday. We cannot change the past, only deal with the present.

The experience of loss and the emotional response attached to loss is impossible to avoid. In dealing with numerous individuals, the thought crossed my mind with one person, *Here is someone who has her grief work perfect, and she somehow has bypassed grief.* As I listened to the information, it was presented in such a way that controlling grief was simply a natural process for them. For me, everything read, taught, counseled, and experienced said this cannot happen, but I was thinking, *Apparently it does.* However, as one session was coming to a close, the actuality of what was happening came to the surface. There it was—denial, brilliantly dressed with all the correct words, expressions, and mannerisms. The survivor had presented herself as "grief free"—that is, she seemed as though she had worked through the grief process and was currently encountering other obstacles in her life that were "completely different from grief." As we spoke, it became evident that this was a denial of death's impact upon her life, and the problems being faced were incorrectly assumed by the survivor as separate from grief. As we would discover, the difficulties were in fact directly connected to the death. The pressure to be well and the desire to be beyond the sorrow or the fear of grieving became grounds for denial. This denial is a method of dealing with life's difficulties by deflecting or avoiding them. Learning new patterns of dealing with grief expression and facing life as it is became the challenge.

This individual who was in denial came seeking help for a different problem that appeared to have little connection to the loss of a spouse and grief. In having her tell her story about recent events, she mentioned, in passing, that her spouse had died and spoke of this as "just another" event in daily life, as if it had no effect upon her. If I had not been listening closely, the mention of this death may have seemed no different than any other event in a busy week. When the story was finished, we began to explore what had happened with her spouse, the preceding illness, the care, the death, and how all of this has affected her life. The effect was "not noticed" because of her emotional blindness to the death. She could not, or would not, allow herself to recognize the death of her spouse and her denial of its impact upon her life. She knew something was wrong but could not identify what it was. Denial can manifest as a complex jumbling of events in which emotional and mental awareness become fogged over, making visibility extremely limited. The fog keeps things hidden with the intention to avoid. The separate problem that brought this woman in for assistance eventually wove its way back to the death of her spouse, into the fog where she was eventually able to disperse the haze.

The loss reaction and grieving are impossible to avoid, just as being disappointed with the cancellation of a much-anticipated vacation or a change of plans after months of planning are losses that we grieve. The accompanying response to loss is the establishing of a self-created pattern of loss reaction. Think of the expression, "They need to get a grip on themselves." The interpretation is to get a grip on the reaction or sorrow displayed. It is wrong to assume that to get a grip on life means that someone should show no expressions or have no expectations, pretending that loss means nothing. Any event that has a deep emotional attachment, that involves love, or that includes a once-in-a-lifetime expectation will produce a response. If you love a particular team and they win, you are excited; and if they lose, you are sad or grieved. We use this same pattern with any significant loss; it follows the outlines already established by life with losses of lesser significance.

Love understands what made the person attracted to you and you to them. Take time to understand yourself, the strengths in your life, and the weaknesses. Locating something to blame is not the goal, but knowing your needs, desires, and what you value is the goal. Know your strong points and your weak points; deciding which things to avoid and things to embrace is a conscience decision. As individuals cross your path, know what you value most. Look for places to meet friends that fit where you are now; this is a choice. Remember that if "love is blind," then desire is deaf and dumb (the desire to be left alone, pulling back into a shell, isolation).

Love, which is sacrificial, is not blind to the sacrifice made. Love allows the truth to be established—the good, the bad, and the not so good. Wrong desires make you willing to pay any price to get what you do not have and to keep what you do not own. Know yourself, and you will find those who will love and appreciate you for who you are. Make friends with those who are comfortable with themselves, with their faults and virtuous qualities. Get to know the complete person, as much as possible, before jumping into an association or friendship. Whether it is going out with a group of friends or meeting a person for lunch, remember that it is just lunch. When I heard the quote "It's just lunch" on television, it was a surprise since I had been using it for years. What better way to meet with a group or an individual than to meet for lunch. It is in a public yet somewhat private setting, and it has a beginning and an end. You have the option to leave immediately after finishing your meal or to sit there for an hour—either way works. You have topics to discuss, such as what your favorite meals and restaurants are and trips you have taken. Love life—it is a gift to be shared. Do not allow anxiety of loss to confine your activity.

Unit 14

Avoidance

When grief stricken, it can appear that no one on the planet is like you. Please note, however, that you are not alone. There are countless individuals going through the exact same experience. The viewpoint held by some in society is that grief should be kept hardly visible, out of sight, with the hope that it will vanish completely. As you are aware, this way of thinking does not work, and the missing grief keeps reappearing. The wound left by loss will not heal by evading it. The key is handling, holding, reviewing, talking, writing, and dealing with whatever has happened and is happening. The goal is to deal with loss but to do so in manageable segments. Initially, there is an inclination to avoid particular thoughts or areas where you had shared experiences with the deceased. We do this by shunning certain areas that keep past memories from arising, but there comes a time when these evasive moves no longer work. Running away from or trying to block certain things is not a bad thing in the beginning. At first, the grief is overwhelming, so it is impossible to sort through everything at once. This avoidance of some things may help in the short time frame, but in time, as you become more resilient, you will be able to deal with them. When the evasive maneuvers started, it was a defense to push these concerns off until a later time, and this is the later time. No matter where you are or what the day brings, there is to be time set aside for dealing with the events of the day, those which were set aside "to be dealt with later."

Avoidance is not the same as denial. If there is a tree in your yard and its leaves are falling, avoidance says, "There is a tree in my yard and its leaves have fallen, but I am not going to rake the leaves until later." Denial declares, "There is no tree, and there are no leaves." Avoiding some things in the grieving process has its virtues, but only for a time. This mourning period is longer, is more difficult, requires more time, expresses more emotions, and expends more energy than ever expected. Grief will surface at the most unexpected places. Most often, what we avoided will rise again.

Grief declares, "Deal with me today or deal with me later, but I will need to be dealt with."

Only the one grieving can know how tragic the event, the loss, or the death really is. Mourning is a personal expression of loss. Life during this time of sorrow can feel uneven, like an out-of-balance washing machine on the spin cycle, rocking and clanging as if it will fall apart. If the washing machine is totally out of balance, it will shut down and the contents will need to be redistributed, or some garments even removed, so the spin cycle will continue. Likewise, the path of mourning will bring its cycles; some of these cycles will work themselves out, and others will cause a shutdown where redistribution is necessary. And some "garments" will need to be removed, set aside for now, and reentered later.

Grief also can bring its times of shutdown when the need for professional help arises for the redistribution of the grief that one carries. This is grief and sorrow at their worst, when the bereaved feels like the life once loved is gone and asks, "How will I make it?" Did I mention that grieving is the hardest thing you will ever accomplish in life? Do not be hard on yourself; no guilt trips are allowed. You survived the experience, and you will make it through the grieving process. There are individuals who love you, and there are individuals you love. At this moment, they are pushed somewhere in the background because of this loss and its impact on daily living. These loved ones will one day be in the forefront of life again, but for now do not burn any bridges that connect your life to others. What is upsetting today may mean little tomorrow. There's no rush, no push, and no guilt trips, no matter who is misrepresenting life. For some, the illustrations will help in bringing a little balance into this spin cycle of grief. For others, stories are of little value. There are many levels and seasons of grief. What does not fit today may fit tomorrow. You are not alone.

Moving from avoidance has an influence on how we speak. Remember that we are not unwinding or undoing the life that you had together. That is impossible. It is today when your loved one is no longer present to stitch together two lives. The story of today is more than the wound caused by yesterday. Life is more than mourning, sickness, or loss. It is the story of relationship, of beginning, of progression, of someone becoming an essential part of whom you are, of arriving at whom you are now. It is in this "wanting to continue" the interweaving of lives that pain of loss arises. It is in this everyday intertwining of life where grief stands up and declares, "We are no longer able to continue the interlacing; one is missing."

Notice the way death is spoken of: "I feel like my life has become unraveled." Now, here we are, flung into this present day, into this unraveling loss experience we call grief. The separation caused by death makes it feel like every stitch we created in a love relationship, every stitch sewn into the fabric of the soul is now creating a piercing hurt as death tries its best to unstitch life. Every memory, every stitch, and every experience brings the reality of death and realities of a hurtful separation—my loved one is no longer here. "I am only one thread, and once there were two." The grief experience feels like we are coming apart at the very seams of our soul. At the very beginning of life together, we never dreamed of a time when one life would end. The focus was on loving and learning how two individuals function as one. The sewing together of life between two was difficult, some more difficult than others. But now we are learning to live life as one. One is a lonely number. This coming back to singleness is the hardest of life events. Pause for a moment and inject this thought—sometime in the future, "what was" will bring comfort to life; this will not happen today but someday. Looking back on what was will have its personal beauty.

Unit 15

Public and Private Grief

In recognizing grief, we become aware of how loss demonstrates itself with two emphases, one that looks upon personal grief expression and the other as public grief expression. Grief expression declares that we hurt over our loss and that it is normal for there to be emotional, physical, mental, and spiritual manifestations of this loss. The loss has both a private and a public reality. They are not the same. What we express in the private places is disclosed only for a select few who understand the grieving process (e.g., crying in the shower, screaming into the pillow, lying around all day, crying continuously, questioning, doubting, etc.). The public does not need to know the specifics of your grief, only that you experience good days and bad days. That is an excellent statement to remember when someone asks, "How are you doing?" The response is simple: "I have my good days and my bad days." It is the truth and, for most who wish to maintain personal contact, it will pacify their need to ask.

In grief, there is an altering of public life. To go on as if nothing happened would create difficulties personally, professionally, and relationally. If there were no expression of loss after the death of a loved one, it would be cause for concern. But if grief is too volatile, such as uncontrolled crying in the workplace, it becomes troubling for those with a "you cannot do that at work" mentality. Individuals have spoken of their superiors' threatening to fire them if they did not keep their mind on their work. Then the other side of the response brings questions like, "Does it not appear odd that they pretend to live life like nothing happened?" Others present the "superhuman" or "superspiritual" approach, saying things like, "Death does not faze me. I pretend they are on a trip," "I buried my loved one and went to work that afternoon—never looked back," or "My loved one is in heaven. Why should I grieve?"

If you are grieving, the public is an area where you are vulnerable because everyone has an opinion, advice, a book, a counselor, or a vitamin, and you are left to sort out what may help in your grief. You cannot please all of them, and most of what they offer will not fit your way of expressing sorrow. An approach for the workplace is to offer simple, general details such as the name of the illness or problem (heart attack), what happened (severe pain in chest), who came (family and friends), what changed (turned my life upside down), and how are you doing (I have good and bad days), and then close the conversation by thanking them for their concern. The events read like a news article minus the emotional attachment to the event. This emotional detachment is for the inquiring individuals who really have no need to know or see the emotional side of your experience. Having a prepared general statement for the majority of people is a good thing. Only one or two individuals qualify for the relational position of receiving full transparency with your grief. These individuals will support you no matter what feelings or statements you express.

Grief is demonstrated by conveying our broken connections. Death has separated our loved ones from life as we know it, and we mourn their loss. Those experiencing grief live in today without their loved ones and with an emptiness that is difficult to define and express, and nothing fills the void. Grief has a constant pull. Memories attract us to the past even though we know life as it was is gone. This emptiness of the present is overwhelming; all other relationships or needs appear to be insignificant. The future in this hollow present feels as shattered as our past.

Unit 16

Fact or Fiction

Fact—we know in our minds that our loved ones have died. Fiction—death does not feel real in our hearts or our emotions; it is as if the separation has not occurred. If humankind were only factual, grief would be over at the cemetery. All the facts line up, as they should; the death, the funeral, and the interment are over; now go on living as if nothing happened. It does not work that way. We are also emotional beings. It takes time for the emotions to catch up with the facts. The anguish of grieving is the emotional separation, the tearing apart of two relationships, separating lives that have intricately grown together. We are familiar with the term "bonds of love," which speaks of love holding people's lives together. In death, these bonds of physical and emotional attachment go through a forced separation. It is hard to picture, but grief is separating and pulling apart present life from past life. To imagine that grief is a healing process is a difficult concept. In a tangible way, this experience of grief will be an affirmation of life that forces us to separate from yesterday. It is our way, the human way of healing.

Unit 17

How Long

A question that is very common among those who are grieving is, "How long will this take?" The hard, abrupt answer is, "It will take as long as it takes." Everyone is different. Every relationship is different. The material you read, the understanding of the grieving process, and the experience of grief all have a part in how long the grieving period lasts. The focus of the information offered through these pages, stories, and illustrations is to support the everyday walk that is experience. "How long?" is a question that focuses on the passage of time as if time will heal the wounds of death and separation. The expression that comes from this opinion is "Time heals all wounds." I would like this to be true, but it is not. If time healed all wounds, then letting time pass would make everything better. But we know of individuals who, twenty or thirty years after a death, are bitter, angry people, emotionally isolated, and confined. Time did not heal their wounds. It will take one year to experience many of the firsts in the grief experience. Will it be over in a year? No. Missing someone you love will last a lifetime, but how they are missed and the way one expresses this absence changes.

Time and working through the wound of grief is how the healing comes. It is somewhat correct that it takes time to heal, but to heal wounds of grief where there are numerous memories and "wells" of tears takes an open, vulnerable effort. Grieving is combining this struggle with time and memories and today's events. It will take a lot of work. Some have stated that working through grief "is the hardest work I have ever done." The grief experience is not just waiting for next year to arrive, when the apparent list of firsts will be behind you. This anniversary arrives with memories of all that took place a year earlier. It has been stated about anniversaries of a loved one's death, "It feels exactly as it did a year ago." The memories of that period come back as if they happened yesterday. The difference lies in the fact that what took months to work through earlier may now take a few days or weeks. The "time heals all wounds" concept asserts that if I

38

can somehow reach a certain date or make it through a certain number of weeks or months, I will be through this remorse and can move on with life. Time is not the healer of all wounds. Healing requires a combination of time, action, labor, memory, grieving, living, and doing, all rolled up in the struggles devoted to living life without the ones we love. So is there a timeline? The time it takes to move through the grieving process is different for each person. I will state this many times. Those experiencing sorrow are similar, yet each one is different. It is important to remember that grieving is not clear-cut, nor is it a steady progression from one place to the next. It is forward, backward, upward, downward, and then forward, backward, upward, downward again, and so on. But you will heal and life will be good again—not today but someday.

There are many occasions when grief will feel like it is going backward instead of forward. That is the reason for emphasizing the importance to be whom you are, where you are with no pushing or pulling to be somewhere else. When I struggle to establish some type of time frame, I do so with months, segments of time that overlap. The first three months, then the second through the fourth months, and so on, overlapping, returning, going forward, feeling like we are stuck, and then moving ahead and going back. The length of years can be one to five or longer or shorter. Some have found the second year to be the year of greatest change. Others have stated that it was in first year. Some require more time, saying, "It was three years before I felt I could go on with life." Should we look for time lines? Will it help? I am a time-conscious individual. I am the person who wants to know how long before we get there and how many miles I need to travel each day to reach my destination. For me, stopping is an option, but one I try not to take. Time lines are important, but taking time is more important than rushing to a finish line that does not exist. We live with death differently, so let the different certainties settle in. There is no rush. There is no push. This is not a race but a day-by-day living, loving, grieving, and believing. When trying to force grief into a schedule, it becomes easy to arrive at incorrect assumptions by applying deadlines to our grief. With the desire to end grief, speed it up, and move on, individuals incorrectly self-diagnose where they are in reference to the date of death, creating a judgment that does not fit and that confines, restrains, and pushes the grieving process. It does take one year to experience many of the firsts that accompany death, so we imagine that the last of such firsts will occur on the first anniversary of the death. However, this may not be the case, so we must take time, with no rush or push, to deal with the difficulties that present themselves, express what we are feeling, express what we are experiencing, and shape these feelings and experiences with memory. We need to bring this reshaping into today's living as we discover that life as it was is a memory and as we figure out life as it is now, in the present, and life for tomorrow, in the future. In grief, life is rolled into a mix that will not hold itself together. Dealing with each event as it arrives or in a timely manner allows us to move through our grief progression. This draft of the grief process provides an outline, minus time, to help relate the grieving process to what is taking place in our lives. We grieve at our own pace.

Unit 18

Finding Help

When grief leaves you emotionally drained and death has eliminated the one you counted on to help with decisions, it is difficult to determine who is there to help with choices. In addition, there is an added stress in being cautious of those offering help. Are they trying to capitalize on your vulnerability, or have they been trustworthy in the past? In the "normal time of your life," this distrust is less likely to happen, but, sad to say, many of us are pushovers for a good story. Before you make any major decisions related to finances, moving, buying, selling, or giving, ask those you trust for their thoughts. Remember, these are only opinions. You make the final decision.

Here is another idea to keep in mind. If anyone brings you an idea, remember that it comes only as one placed on the "table" before you, along with other ideas, just like dishes at supper. The table for this illustration is your kitchen table. The ideas given by others or collected, many or only a few, are all placed on the table. Look at the ideas and discuss the good and the bad aspects of each. You will move them around, and some will appear better than others. The less-appealing ideas are placed off to the side. When there are a top two, then a decision is made as to which of the two is better. This will not be a black-and-white decision; it may be a 51-percent-to-49-percent decision. But it becomes a direction in which to travel, but only as you decide. Once a choice is made, it is always yours to change.

Whenever you take the idea off the table as your choice, it belongs to you. Success or failure lies with you and the reason for the choice. The purpose for keeping the decision with you is that there can be no strings attached. As to owing the originator of the idea, there is no one to blame should it go wrong. There are no strings attached should it be right. There is a decision that needs worked and monitored. If it is not working, then stop, go back to the table of ideas, and see if other ideas can be integrated with this one or change ideas for another course of action and see how that works. If the decision made veers off the intended course, no problem. Go back to the table of ideas with a more complete understanding of what is required. Contact an individual who is an expert in this field to get more information to take into consideration.

As a person who has encountered loss, you are aware that things do not go as planned. But this is not an excuse not to try, and because of your knowledge of change, it will help keep the changing course of grief moving. The changes not only are emotional or relational but may include buying or selling a home, a car, or a lawn mower or even moving to another state. Receiving counsel is a good idea, but everyone has an idea. Many will have a "must do" attached, but in reality, there are very few must-do-now decisions. Be wise. Know that a mandate that sounds like "you must do this my way" needs to be questioned. Do not allow anyone to force you into a decision. This force can come from a telemarketer seeking personal information, a "friend" wanting to add his or her name to your checking account, or a family member wanting only the best for you. Be wise. Do not allow yourself to be manipulated into any decision. You maintain the final say—"yes," "no," or "I need to think on this for a time." Seek information from trusted individuals, organizations, or professionals who will give unbiased information. Seek legal counsel for concerns that deal with property, finances, estates, or wills. Becoming blind to life and the things that need to be accomplished is not an option. Know the reasoning behind your decisions. This is not about giving trust; it is about individuals' earning trust. With this effort, you are gaining understanding for present and future decisions. Remember, you do not give trust. Trust must be earned.

In the process of acquiring information and its discussion, always maintain that you have the final say even if the choice is allowing someone to lead the way in choosing a direction. This is your life, your possessions, and your money; this is for your benefit. Know and understand the decision and possible outcomes, good and bad. Then decide what will be best for you. If it is determined that you do not have the privilege to stop the process, then look for an alternative. You know better than anyone else that life changes, and you have the privilege of change. This choice is yours, even the choice to have certain people involved to help in the decision making. You are not obligated to the originator of an idea. If there are strings attached to ideas, such as that you owe the person who came up with them, then those ideas are probably not in your best interest. Making choices empowers you to continue to make choices. Making wise choices based on information from different sources is accomplished by sorting through facts and opinions. All of this may be new, but it is part of who you are becoming. Seek a couple of different opinions from different sources. It is your life; it has value. If it had no value, then others would not be trying to direct your choices.

Unit 19

Money/Finances

You may question why I would place this topic so close to the beginning. Finances will need immediate attention, and the decisions you make can affect the rest of your life. Be very careful; be very guarded with financial decisions. If you have never cashed a check, balanced a checkbook, or paid a bill, learning how to do these functions will add even more anxiety to the already stressed life of grief. In every death, the bereaved is left without the input of the other. When the bills come due and you have never written a check or done online banking, the "I've never done that before" fear comes knocking at the door. Seek help from the bank or an accountant to aid in accomplishing the weekly and monthly tasks of paying bills. In marriage, two individuals are living one life. When a spouse dies, half or more of the activities accomplished in the household are left undone. Whether it is cooking or putting gas in the car, there are some things that one of you seldom, if ever, did. The area of finances requires security and careful examination carefully by someone who is trustworthy and skilled in special areas. In marriage, generally, one is often more capable than the other at certain tasks, so the duty fell to him or her. If you were not the bookkeeper, the mower of the lawn, or the chef, then these areas create a lot of pressure now that the other is absent.

When there are adult children, sometimes, one or more of them step up to assist. Sometimes this is good, and sometimes this is bad. I have seen occasions when children have emptied the financial accounts of their parent and left them penniless, and I have seen times when loving and caring children have sacrificed their own financial well-being to keep the remaining parent financially solvent. On other occasions, siblings have accused one another of stealing, channeling monies into their own accounts, or buying things for themselves out of the parents' funds. So what is the best way? That is up to you and your family. There is no a one-size-fits-all solution. Be aware that this is not the time to hand over your finances to someone who has had financial problems. You know whom to trust—those who have proven themselves trustworthy. Always maintain accountability. If there is going to be conflict, get an outside accountant, CPA, or bookkeeper to help establish a sound financial strategy. Many times, it is helpful to have a trusted individual with you when seeking counsel to confirm all that is said, and be sure to monitor the process with continued follow-ups. Have investors show you in writing what they promise, and you maintain the final say. Even if you feel that your finances are nothing much to be concerned about, at least have someone help with understanding which bills come monthly and how they are paid. Many workbooks offer help in financial planning and can be found in local bookstores or online.

When making a decision to search for outside help with your finances, it is best to seek out referrals for a particular consultant. The cost must be considered, but you maintain control of the decisions. Do not simply hand over access to your monies to anyone. If individuals in the family disagree with your decisions, have a family meeting and invite the financial advisor or the bookkeeper to explain the benefits of what is provided. This ensures that everyone is aware of what is happening, but it does not mean that everyone will agree with the decision. Perhaps you have heard of conflict management—the word *manage* does not imply resolution of conflicts; it involves managing conflict in such a way that life can continue.

I know a couple who owned their own business. One of them died, leaving this very successful business and quite a substantial death benefit to the surviving spouse. The business was sold, and the surviving spouse relocated to be near her children. Later, one of the children requested a considerable amount of money from her to start his own business. She refused, saying, "I am older. If I invest in your business venture and it fails, I can never recover from this financial loss and will not have sufficient funds for my future." There were no hard feelings, but an understanding was established that the mother was not a lending agency and that when she dies, the estate will be divided among the siblings according to the will. This was quite an impressive lesson, knowing how many parents go bankrupt trying to keep their children financially solvent. This mother is equally generous to all of her children on her terms, not at the children's request. Being wise with one's possessions is being a good steward of all possessions. This wise steward will plan for her own life first and not rely on the goodwill that someone may promise. The ability to handle finances wisely is something all should have or develop, and if that is not your gift, hire someone who will help.

Unit 20

Death Benefit, Lump-Sum Payment, Pension

Perhaps the most challenging financial component to deal with is the lump-sum "death benefit." What a confusing name—"death benefit." How can a loving, grieving person receive a benefit from death? When the policies were written, perhaps they were done with a sneer or a joke like, "You're going to get *what* when I die? I am worth more dead than alive." The unthinkable has come to pass, your loved one has died, the policies are cashed, and here is this money paid to you because of the death. The arrival of these funds can be overwhelming, not because the amount is so great but because of the reason the funds are dispersed. Some have torn the check in half, saying, "I would rather have my loved one than the money." That is true, but it is a misinterpretation that creates these feelings. The thought that this is being paid for someone's death is groundless; the term "death benefit" is a misnomer. These are survival benefit intended to keep you financially solvent without your loved one. It is a hard fact, but it takes money to live, and if you have planned for this day, the money received will be a great help. For many, there is no money or the money will not be enough to maintain life as it was. Either way, the feelings are conflicting—the money will help, but wrongful guilt clings to the benefit.

Survivors have given this money many unjust names, none of which are appropriate. The truth concerning money received as a survivor benefit is that it is money invested with an insurance company or at work that promised a payout at a certain time. It is money invested monthly over many years, and now the disbursement of that policy has occurred. It is the same as if money were placed in the stock market or a certificate of deposit in a bank. The money received at this time is the result of paying a self-imposed bill to a company that invested it for you until a later time. You or your loved one received and paid a life insurance notice each month or each year as a provision for the surviving spouse, child, or estate. This policy, or "survivor's benefit," came into being because of planning and investing. There was a plan in place so that, should one die, the selected individual, estate, or organization would be the benefactor. A simple explanation is that the insurance company takes a gamble. It wants policy holders to pay into a plan for many years while it continues to invest the money received so that when the policy is surrendered at death, it will have made more money than it has to pay out as a benefit. All of this is initiated by a desire to ensure that if one income disappears, there will be adequate money for the survivor to maintain his or her lifestyle.

One young family I know invested in a life insurance policy, and the next month, one of them was killed in an auto accident. The surviving spouse and children were grateful for the wise decision the parents had made. In another situation, the working spouse had opted out of the pension plan at work and died at age fifty-five. The surviving spouse went to the company to collect on her husband's benefits only to find out that there was nothing. The death benefit plan offered by the company allowed her to receive a little more than his weekly salary. It was at this point that the spouse had to enter the workforce even though she had never held a job outside of the home. It became a financial struggle for her to survive and was a grievous disappointment.

You can also view the money received after a spouse dies as if you had paid a monthly bill to a safe-deposit box located in the bank. At the time of death, the spouse goes to the bank to open the safe-deposit box. This is your money paid to a box and intended to be withdrawn when the other dies. These funds were always part of the family finances. It is money saved for this time of life. These funds are to be use wisely, as was the intent when the plan was established. Some individuals have an incorrect view of this benefit and unwisely give the money away to the point that they lose everything they own. Also, such disdain for the money received will lead to foolish financial decisions. People who were not careful were taken advantage of by unscrupulous individuals, leaving the bereaved drained of all of their financial resources. Guilt played a major role in the loss of these resources. One such individual lost everything, including his home, mainly because he was uncomfortable with the money he had received.

Another area to be concerned with is the estate you leave to your children, family members, or friends, or perhaps you choose to leave some of yours to an organization. Make sure your wishes are stated specifically. Clear desires stated in a will can avoid confusion and hard feelings. Siblings and money—or anyone and money—can make for a volatile experience if not well handled. In one situation, a parent had a will that equally divided the estate, but she later became upset with an in-law. So she took another child to the attorney and wrote the disputed in-law and child out of the will. Years later, the parent would speak of the change and express sorrow for this action, but she never changed the will. One child got everything, and the one who was her primary caregiver received nothing.

The importance of being wise in your financial dealings cannot be overemphasized. Wills and trust funds are only two of the avenues through which you can transfer wealth. Everything we own is one day going to belong to someone else. It is in our best interest to be wise in how we use our funds and how they are transferred. I once saw a license plate holder that read, "I am out spending my kids' inheritance." No matter what the slogan, it is yours until you give it away. We are to be wise stewards of everything we possess—our time, our talents, our monies, and our prayers. They are gifts. All will be remembered; let us be remembered as wise stewards of them.

Unit 21

God and Grief

At the heart of grief is also our belief in God. The understanding of God's character will have a significant impact on grief. The greatest misunderstanding with faith in God is making God in our image, after our likeness. God is often perceived as a benevolent grandfather deity who thinks and acts and gives as a glorified human grandfather with no limit to his resources, seeking only to make his grandchildren love him. Then, when this god does not come through as expected, we ask, How can he be present everywhere? How can God know everything or speak and create? Why does God permit death? How could a loving God …? It is around these questions, these greater-than-life mysteries of God, that our life and faith revolve. My personal declaration of grief and God is, "I have a very real problem, and I have a very real God. I do not know why things happen as they do, but I know God is with me." Life's difficulties and faith in God merge together through the expectations that every problem finds a solution in God and that God is at work through every problem. Note that not all things or problems originate with God. God is not the author of confusion. He is not the author of evil, doubt, despair, pain, or suffering. It is impossible for God to have a negative thought of you. How will the two—the real problem and the real God—merge to bring resolution to life?

Several situations in the Bible can be helpful. In trying to make sense of life, the first step is to consider all the good that has happened in your life. Consider how this good came to pass and the circumstances that needed to align in making good happen. The arrangement of good is beyond understanding or even the best-laid plans. If making sense of all the good that has transpired becomes impossible, there certainly cannot be a mortal understanding, a human perspective, that makes sense out of death. Trying to make sense out of something that makes no sense is *nonsense*!

A perspective that our nature would devise is, "I deserve good." If that logic is followed and then bad things happen, the "I deserve this" mentality is shattered by "I am not so bad to deserve this. Look at what I have done." Do not allow the nonsense of some disheartened individuals rob you of your greatest supporter, God, and your belief in His Word. No matter where you are in this grief experience, the goal is to deal with grief in a way that leaves no area of life hidden from the present and to remember in a healing way the love of your life and the dreams left unfinished. God has never left; He is here.

To see God as the center of life is a special viewpoint in which every aspect of living revolves around Him. We cannot comprehend death, loss, or the reason that our loved ones are gone. In our line of sight, death makes no sense. We know that God is not caught off guard by events as if He did not see them coming. But here in God, we are assured that life is in every breath—not our breath but the breath of God. The continuation of life after breathing stops lies in the breath of God, which cannot be smothered in death, for those we call dead are still alive. "It stands to reason, doesn't it, that if the alive-and-present God who raised Jesus from the dead moves into your life, he'll do the same thing in you that he did in Jesus, bringing you alive to himself? When God lives and breathes in you (and he does, as surely as he did in Jesus), you are delivered from that dead life. With his Spirit living in you, your body will be as alive as Christ's!" (Romans 8:10–11 The Message, MSG).

The objective for today and tomorrow is to embrace both our faith and our grief. Life as we know it has changed, not only for us but also for the deceased; they are with God, who is the giver of life. In grief, embrace the memories; know that in time, the memories that now bring pain will one day bring comfort. These memories of life, the recollections that brought purpose and meaning to life, are not gone. They are not erased. The ones we shared these moments with have gone to their eternal home. Until that day we transition from life to life, we live here with memory, with our present loved ones, and with a divine purpose. Some doubt that there is any further purpose to living now that death has come to their loved ones, but we have a purpose or we also would be in heaven. Life will be good again, perhaps not today but someday. God and we together will make life make a difference. God has not changed. The same God who comforted Abraham when his wife Sarah died is the same God who is comforting us.

Unit 22

God with Us

The understanding we have of God will bring comfort or will bring distress. I am referring to each person's knowledge of or personal awareness of God's interactions with humankind. The "distressing" perception believes God to be vengeful, and if that is the case, then the death of a loved one is caused by God's getting even for a past failure. The distressing view questions whether God is one of unfailing love because He failed—separation is not loving. In this view, God is somewhere distant from earth; He is not involved and does not care. Those who believe there is no God consider death a proof of noninvolvement since, somewhere in the process of a loved one's dying, a request was offered, a prayer was given, a bargain presented, and this god did not take the exchange of "my life for theirs." Therefore, to their minds, God does not exist. In our reasoning, any being would take the bargain, exchanging a strong life for a frail, dying one. Such thinking or reasoning is positioning God as almost just a little higher than us, in our image, in our likeness, a human god who is a master of a slave market, looking for a better deal, a stronger physique than the frail. Attempts to negotiate with the Almighty as if God were looking for an exchange or in need of filling a quota, with little regard for which body is there, leave the barterer frustrated, hurt, and in disbelief.

Life is more than dying, and dying is not the end of life. Our bargains are really a way of expressing love and value to the one who is passing. God is not rejecting the bargain offered when one is dying; it is simply that person's time to go home. It is not age, love, poorness, richness, intelligence, feebleness, or healthiness that wins the death lotto. It is just that we live life until we live again. These are but a few thoughts some have offered to demonstrate their "logical" rhetoric about death and God, concluding that because God does not take the exchange they offer, they choose to punish God by not believing. The understanding we have of God will bring comfort or distress. What is your assessment of God considering all that has happened? Is it a distressing concept? What is it that God did or did not do that makes God so distressing? Take a few moments to write out the evaluating thoughts, ideas, and events that supported this decision.

There are many views of life and death and God. The following are some thoughts concerning what the Scriptures declare of the character of God and His involvement with life. (This is not an extensive affirmation.) The declaration "God is with us" is made in a biblical term, *Emmanuel*. Matthew 1:23 (King James Version, KJV) says, "Behold, a virgin shall be with child, and shall bring forth a son, and they shall call his name Emmanuel, which being interpreted is, God with us." This is only one of many texts presented in references found in the Old Testament and the New Testament concerning God's being with us.

A few thoughts—events cannot change truth. It is impossible for God to not be with us. It is part of His divine character. He is omnipresent, present everywhere at the same moment. The question really is not in God's lack of presence but in what appears as His lack of intervention. The greatest privilege of life is to know that we are safe and secure in the hand of God. God has waited a lifetime to welcome His children home. Psalm 116:15 (KJV) says, "Precious in the sight of the Lord is the death of his saints." The question of life and death is settled for those who have died believing in Christ. They are in heaven. But for us, the questions and feelings of loss continue. From our place of understanding, death has the appearance of God's not responding appropriately to a specific request. The shadow of death has overshadowed life, and in this place of the shadow of death [Psalm 23:4: "Yea, though I walk through the valley of the shadow of death, I will fear no evil: for thou art with me; thy rod and thy staff they comfort me" (KJV)] we see no purpose in our loved one's dying, not now.

Grief is what we feel as we pass through the shadow of death. It is in this shadow of death called grief that God has promised to protect and guide us (His rod and staff). The promise is recorded in Hebrews 13:5 (KJV): "For he hath said, I will never leave thee, nor forsake thee." In God's continuous presence, He is with us, and those who have died are with God. We may never understand in this lifetime why the lives of our loved ones left us, but in faith, we know that it is only for a time and that we will be with them again. This truth does not erase pain, but it comforts us. It accompanies us in our time of sorrow and through every aspect of grieving. This is where God, life, faith, and death merge, God with us. I have a very real loss, and I have a very real God. He comforts me.

Unit 23

Forgiveness

The "not so obvious," hidden parts of grief are those memories that have wounds attached. These wounds may have been intentional or unintentional, but both will require forgiveness. Unforgiveness is not an option. In the real world, relationships do not consist of two identically verbal individuals who talk through and work through all obstacles and disagreements in a kind, loving, caring way, giving preference to the other, speaking openly of life, and finding healing to all hurts. Most have had conflict at some time, even in the most perfect of relationships.

We do not live in a perfect world. If it were perfect, we would be the ones asked to leave. Many times there is "stuff" that is not resolved before a loved one dies. This stuff has its own emotional injuries that have led to our creating barriers one brick, one hurt at a time, that were not dismantled before the loved one's death. The best way to pull apart this barrier is to work through the hurts with the loved one before it's too late, but many find this too difficult and the time to short. The things you wanted to say remained unsaid. Now this stuff occupies your heart in a hurtful way.

As with most sensitivity walls, construction took place at a time when situations created friction, and it was easier to take each hurt and place it in the wall; after all, it was only one brick, one problem. At the time, it was decided that the hurts were not that important, not worth the conflict it would create to try and resolve them, so we put them off until later. If the loved one dies before the problems are resolved, there can be wounded memories, which feel like resentment or anger toward the loved one, and then we feel guilty about feeling hurt.

Forgiveness is about forgiving ourselves as much as it is about forgiving others. Some write a letter to the deceased, take the letter to the cemetery to read, and bury or burn it there. Some have let off balloons as visible prayers ascending to their loved ones. Forgiveness is letting go of the pain and the hurt. Forgiveness is not about trying to fool yourself into thinking that certain events were not that important. Regardless of the severity of the wound, from a scratch to a broken heart, forgiveness is the only option. Take the real pain to a real place. For some it is the cemetery, where they request forgiveness and leave it there. Much of the forgiveness desired has already happened. The loved one understood your personality and gave his or her forgiveness by remaining in the relationship for the good it offered, which is the love shared together. The healing walk is remembering the past and dealing with it in the present. Grieving takes on an expression of its own that overrides what were once considered the normal aspects of everyday life. The path of grief is one that experiences loss, deals with today, and wonders if tomorrow will be survivable. This is an intense period, but it will change with time. Struggles will come and go, but we continue through each day, dealing with yesterday's memories and today's sorrows, and questioning whether tomorrow will come.

Unit 24

Questioning God

I have heard it said, "We should never ask God why," surmising that God is above questioning and life above understanding. Of course, the avoidance of asking is based on having faith. My personal observation is that this is one of those "should" statements that serves to manipulate hurting individuals into shying away from asking questions for which we, in our finite perspective, have no adequate answers. If you are forbidden from asking, religious scholars do not have to try to find an acceptable answer. The answer becomes, "I do not have an answer." So if the perfect response for the questions concerning death become off limits, as if "godly people trust and do not ask God questions" we remain in our frustration, thinking that God hurt us intentionally. The correct way to proceed is that you should ask God any question that crosses your mind. People of faith are not to check their brains at the front door of the church to believe in God. Show me a relationship without dialogue, and I will show you that there is no relationship. The dialogue begins with prayer and is a two-way conversation through the Scriptures.

Prayer is conveying to God what He already knows and then listening for what God has already said. Is that confusing? Think of it this way—God knows all things, possesses all knowledge, and will never say anything that contradicts the Scripture. God knows all things, and the answer lies within the Scriptures. The problems lie in combining "religious" traditions with the limitations of human sight, mixed with the best of intentions, and the result is a diluted concept of God. Much of what we do or do not believe about God are misconstrued ideas taken out of context and presented as someone's certainties. Remember, in prayer, I am releasing to God all the frustrations, fears, questions, and agonies surrounding my life, as well as studying the Scripture, knowing God's Word, and allowing this Word to speak to my life and guide my understanding.

For this to happen, there first must be a relationship, which begins by asking Jesus Christ to forgive us of our sins and enter into our lives. From this relationship flows an understanding that God is with me; my sins are forgiven; all my past thoughts, words, and deeds are forgiven; and my life is alive in God. From the relationship and the situations of life come our questions, our prayers, and our reading the Bible (start with the gospel of John), seeking the divine in our human struggle of life and death. The answer to prayer is not an instant text message from the Almighty, although we would prefer this to waiting. The disclosure to our prayer often comes over time as the healing process takes place. The reason we study the Scriptures is to know the author. Knowing the author becomes our source of life. Jesus is the Word made alive and living among us, and from this life we receive instructions on how to live our lives with the strength to make changes.

Why should I communicate to God what He knows? Prayer is more than questioning or a handing over of hurt, fear, and frustration; it is a sharing of our hearts. This sharing, this prayer, involves giving our desires, hopes, and expectations and a release of our faith that reaches beyond the limitations of human intervention. The answer returns in the form of that "still small voice" (1 Kings 19:12 KJV): "And after the earthquake a fire; but the Lord was not in the fire: and after the fire a still small voice." It reveals promises identified in Scripture that declare strength, guidance, going, standing, waiting, peace, comfort, love, provision, and so on. The distinction of belief, of faith, is the acceptance that no matter what happens, God is with us, giving us strength for this day. How much faith is required? We must have enough faith to ask and then not betray our request by second-guessing life. Be at peace in our hearts. When I am at peace, I can see things more clearly and understand more deeply. God and I make a great team.

No matter how much faith we possess, there is a time to die and a time to mourn (Ecclesiastes 3:2 and 4 KJV). We do so in the security that death cannot conquer life and that nothing can separate us from God's great love. When we ask why, it actually is a statement of faith about what was expected and did not occur. The *why* question implies that we believed in something different from what took place. *Why* also indicates a belief that someone is in control, a belief that someone is looking out for our good.

Death is a separation from physical life but not a separation from God. In fact, death is our going home. We pass from life to life.

With an examination of *why*, there is a need to stop and consider what was expected. Were the expectations expressed in prayer unrealistic? In considering the answer, you may think, *Is it unrealistic to want life to continue as it was, a life with love and joy? What makes a life with purpose and promise so impractical that we would not request divine intervention to maintain it?* Not asking, praying, requesting, or begging for our loved ones to live would be a failure. We make a list of reasons and desires why our loved ones should not die. In each of our lives, we live without knowing when death shall come to claim a body, but death cannot claim what is not death's to own. God gives life. He is the breath of life, and life is His, not to take but to receive home to His place called heaven. When speaking of a car accident in which a child was killed, the child's parent was questioning whether the child had suffered before dying. The autopsy revealed that the child had died from blunt-force trauma and had probably died instantly. The thought that came to me in that moment was that when the child was flung headlong into the crash, everything of life found itself caught in the hands of Jesus, perhaps like one falling and not hitting the ground but being caught by God, safe from harm, alive in heaven, alive in Jesus.

The Bible says, "So teach us to number our days, that we may apply our hearts unto wisdom" (Psalm 90:12 KJV). Death is inevitable, so we are to live as if it may come today but still make plans to live for a lifetime. That is an easy statement but hard to do. If this were our last day, what would we say or do? We would make sure all hurtful areas were forgiven. We would tell the people we love how much they mean to us. We would encourage others and build relationships that would outlive our physical existence. Instead of waiting for the last day, we need to live every day as a personal day of value. This philosophy is more than a push for a good finish as we see death's arrival; because of a love for life and a love of others—and a love for God—we live well. These thoughts move us to touch individuals throughout life. This does not mean that we should "give everything away." The meaning is in being wise with our lives. Life is a gift to be shared. We have only a certain number of days. Be wise in how every day is lived. Be wise with all you possess, a good steward of all that you have, which includes your love, your words, your touch, and your days.

You may wonder, *If God has not answered my requests in the past, why would He help me now with my present request?* This is a great question. Often when prayers are not answered as we expect, disappointment, pain, anger, and frustration surface, as if God did not hear or He does not care. We become angry because we are hurt, disappointed in what is perceived to be rejection. We were expecting and believing in a different outcome, and it did not happen. The anger felt is a response to being hurt on many levels, frustrated with life, and even fearful of what may happen next. Faith is a reality of something desired and expected but not yet seen (Hebrews 11:1). Life is about living. Until we live again, we receive security in the Word that life is eternal. Death will come to everybody, but life will never cease. Life cannot be scattered into nonexistence. Life is not a drop of water falling into an ocean of nothingness. The disbelief arrives with a single focus: "my" desire is not worthy of God's involvement. In our lives, there is a divine plan subject only to personal choice. With choice comes the ability to believe or not believe. He helps us now with the assurance that we discover in His character that life is not over at death and that separation is temporary. We live until we live again.

It is from the reality of life that we pray to the giver of life, Jesus Christ, to intervene and halt physical death. We make this prayer because Jesus has conquered death, hell, and the grave. God has given hope in death, He has given hope to life, and it is from this hope that prayer is expressed. Life is the treasured gift that we desired to keep intact just as it has been. It is from this treasuring of life that prayer is inspired, giving inspiration and direction to our prayers. It is like looking through a prism where we see color and light but have little concept of what the rotating picture means. The stability that arises from life, love, death, grief, and faith is the knowledge that in God is eternal life. What greater assurance can we have than the ultimate answer to our question—"My loved one is alive and well in heaven"? The rearranging of life to fit my expectations, what I resolved for God to accomplish, did not happen. This request is not a failure. My request is an offering of love for life, of a valued relationship with the deceased, and an expectation from God. The outcome is beyond our understanding but not beyond our belief. God was there in the past, He is here in this moment, and He is there in the future.

Unit 25

God's Sorrow

It is challenging to conceive of God experiencing human emotions, especially sorrow. That God somehow experiences loss, sorrow, and suffering, that He would have an understanding of and a connection to grief, and that He could in some way possess empathy and compassion does not fit most concepts of God. Humans logically wonder how or even why an all-powerful God would allow Himself to identify with creation or to experience this agony of death. The following presents one aspect of Scripture that depicts God and His experience of sorrow. The intent is to convey how God the Father, God the Holy Spirit, and God the Son—Jesus Christ—know firsthand about the pain, suffering, agony, and sorrow that is part of the human experience. The prophet Isaiah wrote of this sorrow and separation.

> The servant grew up before God—a scrawny seedling, a scrubby plant in a parched field. There was nothing attractive about him, nothing to cause us to take a second look. He was looked down on and passed over, a man who suffered, who knew pain firsthand. One look at him and people turned away. We looked down on him, thought he was scum. But the fact is, it was *our* pains he carried—*our* disfigurements, all the things wrong with *us*. We thought he brought it on himself, that God was punishing him for his own failures. But it was our sins that did that to him, that ripped and tore and crushed him—*our sins!* He took the punishment, and that made us whole. (Isaiah 53:2–6 MSG)

Isaiah gives us a glimpse of Jesus, "a man who suffered, who knew pain firsthand."

The disclosure presented in Scripture states that God has a firsthand understanding of loss, pain, and grief. God knows the anguish; the tears;

the ache; the feeling of aloneness; and the intense feelings of separation, rejection, and abandonment. Human insight tries to place God above such feelings as if they are impossible for the divine to identify as personal. We see this separation, aloneness, and agony of death with Jesus as He takes upon Himself the sin of humanity. He willingly became the Lamb of God, who takes away the sin of the world. (see John 1:29). John the Baptist identifies Jesus as the "Lamb of God." We know of the anguish of Jesus, of this separation that took place as Jesus hung on the cross: "And about the ninth hour Jesus cried with a loud voice, saying, Eli, Eli, lama sabachthani? that is to say, My God, my God, why hast thou forsaken me?" (Matthew 27:46 KJV). Here, on the cross, Jesus takes upon himself the sin of humanity. He expresses His sorrow at being forsaken and abandoned. He is experiencing personally the separation that accompanies wickedness. This text speaks of not only the separation of physical death but also of His abandonment by the Father, which he personally accepts as He receives the sin of humankind upon Himself. God knows all about our sorrow.

The torment of Jesus is spiritual as well as physical. Jesus's death is one of parting from God the Father as He becomes the sin sacrifice, as He takes upon himself what rightfully belongs upon humankind. This comes with a price—God the Father turns away from Him. This agony of separation from the Father is one that believers in Jesus Christ will never experience. Here in Christ on the Cross is the profound impact of iniquity and the agony of separation that it causes. When our loved ones died, the separation that we grieve is only a dim reflection of the separation experienced by Jesus. Jesus is taking upon himself the separation that accompanies the collective impact of sin, which is eternal death, eternal separation from God, which is something no believer in Christ can experience. Jesus understands the agony of loss and parting from the love of our life. God's love for each of us accepts upon Himself all the failures and mistakes, the breaking of His commands, and the total sin of humankind and bears these upon Himself as He hangs upon the cross in our place. God in Christ knows firsthand what dying physically involves, the pain of separation, and the sorrow of death and of grieving. God is aware, personally aware, of sorrow. Jesus promises to comfort those who sorrow. Matthew 5:4 (KJV) says, "Blessed are they that mourn: for they shall be comforted." God knows and identifies with our sorrow. I pray that the hands nailed to the cross hold and heal your broken heart.

There is no quick fix to grief, no magic eraser or special appeal that takes sorrow away, and no guilt trip that "someone else sorrows more." But knowing that we are not alone in walking this path because God walks with us and feels our pain and our mourning becomes a comfort. God is not the originator of death or the sorrow that it brings. We know that life contains joys and sorrows. We are now aware that God knows what we feel and that He is with us each step we take. I am not alone. God is with me. He makes alive His truths, which bring comfort and strength. I am safe in the arms of my heavenly Father, and my loved one is safe in the arms of our heavenly Father.

Unit 26

Personal Space

C reate your own personal space where you are free to be yourself and to speak or write of what has happened and what is happening. One such place is where you and God are alone. We come into this place seeking nothing but closeness with God. Some have spoken of taking communion every day, consecrating the bread and the juice to God as they remember His love for the world, His love for us. Let it be a sacred time. Be still in this place, meditating on Christ and His adoration of you, His sacrifice, His resurrection, and His presence with you. If you have favorite passages in the Bible, read them and think of God and His divine favor upon your life. If the time is five minutes or five hours, there is no rush and no push—you just want to be close to God.

The personal space originates with you and your need. This other personal space is not so much about the space that surrounds you but the place where you feel comfortable to be you. It can be with a trusted friend, with a professional counselor, while taking a simple walk around the block, or perhaps alone with your journal, writing thoughts at the kitchen table. Whatever the space is, remember that it is a place for you and your thoughts and your feelings. They are important. Take time to think, to remember, and to write them or talk of them, but most of all value them.

I think of when I was a kid with my bow and arrow, trying to shoot the arrow into the clouds. The arrow would fly up out of sight, but it never stuck. It always came back to the ground. Thoughts can be like clouds; they come and go, and you wonder where they went. They disappear as if they were never there. When I shot the arrow into a tree, it stuck. Bringing thoughts to paper gives them substance; they materialize. The thoughts are held, looked at, read, refined, and if you are so inclined, shared with others. Write as if you are the only one who will ever read these words. Let the words flow as a stream pouring from your heart, cascading over the stream bed of your mind, flowing onto the paper through your fingertips. Journaling is a release for what is on the inside seeking expression. Whether you write pages or just a few words, it is your way of expressing that counts. Be at ease with yourself. This is about you—not necessarily the "cascading" of words but your experiences, good and bad. Honestly transcribe whatever enters your mind, with no worries about spelling, grammar, periods, or commas. Write. Express the thoughts that come to mind, giving them a place on the pages of the journal. This openness to expression, the flowing, will create attitudes of openness, which liberates other memories. Personal space creates an openness toward your feelings and thoughts. Remember that what you feel today is important. It appears and disappears like the clouds. Needs will change, thoughts will adjust, and tomorrow will come. But what you wrote today will be remembered and read tomorrow. Grief fluctuates. It gives the impression of being a constant, but it vacillates. What is helpful now may only be so for this moment, and tomorrow's need may be something new. Tracking the changes by journaling will help in seeing the fluctuation and the variation that comes on this grief journey.

Expression is important. Without it, we are in danger of stuffing and holding things in, like damming a river where no outlet exists. The water behind the dam will reach a level where it cannot be contained. It will find a way over, around, under, or through, and the dam will burst. The old cliché of "put a cork in it" does not apply to grief. Every relationship has its positive and negative aspects; be free to express both. To pretend that life was lived without a negative experience places a lot of pressure on the bereaved to recollect only certain qualities, creating in time overflowing stress. When people die, they do not become saints, perfect in all ways. You may have heard people say, "You can't speak ill of the dead." If the person who knows them best, you, is forced not to speak truthfully of the deceased, this becomes the cork in your bottle, the dam with no outlet. The point here is not how good or bad the deceased was but how you, the bereaved, offer yourself approval to speak of the deceased. *What will people think of me if I say what she was really like when no one was around?* you may think. If the image of the deceased in public was different from the one at home and your life has memories with pain attached, it is important that these memories find healing. Find a place to vent and spill over without destroying the good. Seeking a professional to help heal these wounds can be a safe way to relieve the pain. If you choose to stuff the events by not speaking or writing of these truths, they become the dam with no outlet. Eventually, the dam will burst. We are human, and we exhibit human frailties. We are not perfect. In writing a flowing journal, we portray life in its context, the "what happened" prior to and after the circumstances written took place. Life in context is a personal history with you being the storyteller. The story is written through your eyes. We are to speak the truth in context. Life out of context is not a dream but a nightmare. Every day was its own adventure in which life, love, death, grief, faith, failures, and successes were sown together into a story remembered, a personal history of life beginning together all the way to the last words of today's "journal."

II. Section Two

How Bad can this Get

Unit 27

Managing Grief

Managing grief is like managing the weather; just wait a few moments and it will change. We manage the weather by making personal adjustments to the weather, not the opposite. When it rains, you take an umbrella; when it is cold, you wear a coat; and when it is hot, you wear shorts. You manage the weather by preparing for what the weather is and adjusting your life to meet the daily weather conditions. Indoors, we control the temperature by setting the thermostat, but outdoors, we have a thermometer that tells us what the temperature is. You manage grief by preparing for what grief is to you. When I lived in Northern Maine for a few years, the winters were brutal. One year we experienced a six-week period when the temperature never made it above zero, but there was a man who wore only a cotton T-shirt and pants—no jacket, hat, or gloves. When temperatures are below zero, I am cold even with my winter coat, hat, and gloves on, yet he stood there in his T-shirt and said, "I never get cold." Everyone is different, even in managing his or her response to the weather. We manage grief by preparing for what it means to us. The longer our grief continues and the more we deal with the emotional, physical, and spiritual aspects of loss, the greater the possibilities become of being able to set the temperature and of being able to govern our responses to the daily situation. This will require time and a lot of effort.

Unit 28

Death

Death, demise, disease, loss, injury, abandonment, parting, robbery, fire—in any of these situations, a great loss has taken place. The physical and emotional separation of death has collided with life, and grief has begun. Unwelcomed and unwanted, death has come like a thief, leaving you with the responsibility of dealing with heartbreak. Loss has crashed into the life we once knew, leaving us with wreckage that we are responsible for rebuilding. Like a bomb, the grief experience has exploded the normal routine of life, leaving it in rubble and leaving us shattered, searching, questioning, and wondering if there is a way to pick up the pieces. I am sure you noted the expressive words *collided, crashed,* and *exploded*; the intent is to display how destructive death is when it happens. These are the words used by grieving individuals to explain what they felt happened to their lives. This picture of grief breaking in on life is the beginning of the grieving process, with the words describing the uncontrollable events and emotions, the nonstop thoughts, and the aching physical experience that begins when a significant loss occurs, when momentous loss disrupts and fragments one's life. This is not your normal disappointment or "rainy-day feeling." Grief comes in overwhelming waves that barely give you time to catch your breath before another wave breaks upon you. The force of the wave pushes you downward beneath the surface and sends you bouncing along the bottom like a rag doll, struggling and reaching for another breath. A sense of hope arises as you roll onto shore realizing that you are alive, although bruised, scraped, covered in sand, shocked, and questioning what has just happened. *I never saw that coming*, you think. If you have ever been to the ocean and stood in waist-high or shoulder-high water, jumping into the waves as they roll toward the shore, you may understand being caught off guard. "Everything was fine," you might relate later. "I just turned my back for a moment, and this wave from out of nowhere came crashing upon me." With death, this experience has left life forever changed, with you sitting on life's shore looking out on the sea and questioning, "Where did this come from?"

Death can be understood as part of life, as is any significant loss such as the death of a dream, physical limitations after an accident, the loss of a limb, the end of an old way of life, separation, divorce, miscarriage, illness, robbery, fire, flood, loss of a job, or any significant change to what was the normal way of life. While loss is experienced in a varied manner, the information presented here returns to dealing with loss from the perspective of death; in a sense, all loss is a form of death to what was or what was expected. These previously mentioned losses are a death to a former way of life and have similar grief responses that relate to the grief experience of a loved one's death. If you read these pages and the death of a loved one is not your starting point, perchance you will see the similarities. Grief is the wounded experience and expression of sorrow associated with the loss. Grieving is often a very personal expression exposed as sorrow relating to severing connections. Grieving is an experience all will face but seemingly few understand. As many of you have become aware, grieving is an experience many in our society try to avoid.

Unit 29

Grief and the Holidays

Many booklets and pamphlets share ideas as to what someone who is grieving could do during the holidays. The goal is to have a plan. Do not allow the day to arrive assuming someone will call or invite you to be with them. Many of those whom you may anticipate making a call probably feel you want to be alone or that someone else has invited you to be with them. Make plans and speak with family or friends; no matter how you think you will feel, make a plan. You can always leave early or cancel, but last-minute arrangements may not come together, leaving you in a very lonely place. Another thought for the holiday seasons is to keep the old traditions or make new ones. Either way, it is your choice, and you can change next year. If the decision is made, do not change it. During the holiday when all are present, take time to recollect; have someone pause and remember when the deceased was here and share memories. Do not pretend the deceased never existed or was not a part of this time. Mentioning their name, what they did, and how special they were will break through the anxiety that some may feel. This is important for both adults and children. There will be sad tears, happy tears, and laughter, but making time to remember will help everyone once again feel close and part of the gathering. Do not spend the entire gathering as a memorial, but take time to remember. For you, the bereaved, this period of grieving may encompass the entire day, but not everyone has the same level of relationship. Investing what you are with those you love is irreplaceable.

Unit 30

The Path

The grieving process can be likened to walking a path. All who grieve will travel this pathway; no one is exempt. The importance is not the length of time or distance traveled but making the journey. The person of interest is you and how you express your grief. The path or journey of grief is one on which the grieving individual is dealing with his or her grief experience. What makes this route so difficult is the unfamiliar territory this path traverses. Many people have never passed this way before or walked through the challenges this path presents. Unfamiliar terrain, a complex course, course adjustments, feeling lost, and making stops all present their own trials. The questions keep coming: "Is this really the way through the grieving process?" "Will I ever feel normal again?" Grief is a walk through the unfamiliar with no concept of which way is out. The "used to be" is gone. Many of the preconceived ideas have fallen by the wayside, and as they do, people come along with ideas and suggestions that make little sense.

Now, along comes this information, perhaps accompanied by other materials, placed in your hands as suggested resources. These materials become a means of help in understanding and handling this path. Always take time to be safe. There is no rush or push to finish. The goal is to deal with, think over, rehash, remember, cry over, and spend time thinking of life as it presents itself on this path. Be patient with the present. You are holding the memory of one who is a treasure in your life. He or she is no longer here, but you revere his or her life and its meaning. The grief path involves reflecting on how this awareness and this person influenced your life in the past and in the present. His or her death creates this path of grief leading into the future. Now, today, we walk the path of grief through the days of life, one step and one day at a time.

In the years I have spent accompanying individuals as they negotiate this path of grief, I have noticed similarities between grieving people. These common places are the divisions or units of this book—points of similarity along the way. The path has many varied marking posts that are important to some but may or may not be relevant to you. It can be like traveling an interstate highway on which there are many signs, but you will know the stop that fits your need. The emphasis is to travel at your own pace, recognizing your particular need. There is no way to rush the process, and tomorrow's experience cannot be crammed into today. You cannot force tomorrow's sand through today's hourglass. Fall will eventually make it to spring, but it will take about three months of winter. The point is that there is no pushing on to the destination. No matter how hard one tries, Monday cannot become Tuesday; Tuesday must arrive on its own. We cannot transport life out of grief. The fastest way to tomorrow is living through and working through today's experiences.

At times, it feels like we will never reach the destination or that the day will never end. The more we walk, the farther away we seem to get, like we are going forward only to lose ground. This trip is one of walking a while and camping often. The camping spots are particular places that just will not let you go. One of the major campsites is guilt—a topic of its own under another heading. This guilt site is often a maze. As we will find out, forgiveness is the map that shows the way back to the path and allowing growth for the future. Camping also involves staying at places where you find agony or sorrow, which are often the places we want to pass by the fastest. They are uncomfortable places. We ask, "Should I not push on?" The answer seems a bit odd, but we probably need to stop and explore the area. These places might be, for example, holding our loved one's clothes or going to familiar spaces that remind us of when we were there together. This is the opposite of a road trip with the family, when if we found surroundings to be disquieting, we would get out of there as soon as possible and make certain not to stop there again. Grief has a way of making the stop a necessity—a traumatic place entered. But when the time comes to get back on the road, the trauma has been dealt with and the journey continues.

My wife and I traveled to Florida a few years ago and arrived late at the motel to which we had called ahead and made a reservation. We discovered that it was so bad that I kept the suitcase closed and slept in my clothes, and early the next morning, we went looking for another place to stay. Grief is different; these places of discomfort, places that we emotionally push away from, often become places that need extra attention. These spaces belong to you. They are not motels that someone else is to care for, but they are your spaces that need to be cared for, your sorrows that need to be comforted, and your questions that need to be answered. Remember, this walk is not about the invented finish line but the journey. This journey of grief is walking through and living day to day, learning how to live again, and dealing with times and seasons and experiences as they arise. Each day will bring its own emotions, feeling, and memories that stem from the day of the week, the month of the year, or the season. As we walk the path, we live, we feel, we talk, we journal, and we take steps forward and backward. We camp on the trail in places we do not like and in places we love, dealing with times and seasons as they arrive. These memories are just a thought away. In grief, we make a journey that was forced upon us by a death we did not want; traveling to a place we do not know on an unfamiliar path we do not want to travel; stopping in unfamiliar, uncomfortable places on a path that appears to never end. No wonder this is difficult. I remember one person saying after I gave this description, "This path sucks!" But there is purpose to the path. This is how we as humans are wired to deal with death; grief is a forced separation. There is a plan behind the way we grieve. We do not know what that purpose or plan is; perhaps someday we will know or understand, but not today. The path called grief will be traveled one step at a time, one day at a time. The difficult stretches and pauses will one day become more manageable—not today, but someday.

Unit 31

Buffers

Buffers are created, protective ideas that help make the impact of death more manageable. In the physical world, they are pads placed around poles or barriers to protect them should a car crash into them. But in grief, buffers are common, especially in the first few weeks or months after a death. We may create buffers to help keep the realization or impact of death at a controllable distance. Our minds and emotions can deal with only a limited amount of trauma, so we can shut down, disconnect, or create buffers to allow the truth to gradually filter through. These actions are normal, but if they extend into years, they need to be addressed. One buffer often used is to think of our loved ones as being on a trip: "It's just like they are working away." The desire is to place the loss in a category of past actions, making the loss appear temporary and more manageable. "I could not bear to think of him not coming home. So I pretend he is on a trip." The normalcy of this buffer is that, in a period of time, the reality of the loved one's not coming home breaks through the buffer. With some individuals, the buffer becomes denial. All conversations of the deceased are in the present tense, to the extent that the bereaved is living in an unreal world as if the deceased were at home in their room and will return shortly. Sometimes the bereaved portrays the deceased as if he or she were just there a moment ago. What makes grieving so confusing is that these conditions normally occur in the first few days or even months after the death, but when they continue beyond this initial time, help is needed. Those who live in this denial will cover up their make-believe worlds, presenting the "things are fine" appearance. All of their family and friends are pleased that this "grief thing" is going so well. This can last until the one-year, five-year, or ten-year mark, and then family or friends finally decide something is not right. They need help.

Unit 32

"How Are You Doing?"

People in general have little knowledge of what goes on in the grieving process, as if bereavement were a top-secret task hidden from view of the public. We know people die. The newspaper has obituaries listed every day, but understanding the grief process appears to be a different story. Seeing bereaved individuals out at functions, church, the grocery store, or the theater is seeing them in their better moments, their getting-out-of-the-house moments, or the "better get some food in the house" moments. These individuals face the same questions and comments as you when they venture out in public: "How are you doing? You look really good." Their unspoken response is usually, *If you only knew how I felt on the inside.* The responses they give often contain a lie—"I am doing fine"— because they do not want to tell the truth about how bad grief is and they don't want people to think something is wrong with them. Remember, there *is* something wrong; the love of this person's life has died. If you are the bereaved, be kind to yourself. Do not lie to yourself, and do not lie to others. A simple statement can be, "I have my good days and my bad days." That is the truth. This question "How are you doing?" is not a real question; for most, it is a greeting that carries the same value as "Hello." Remember that it does not require a soul-searching response. It's often asked by acquaintances who are sympathetic to your present state and desire information about your condition—those who want to know but do not want to know. One such question caught a bereaved individual at a moment when everything had just "fallen apart." A friend approached and asked, "How are you doing?" The bereaved started to "cry uncontrollably," and the person who had asked apologized and walked away. The bereaved felt "terrible about losing it," but from where I sit, the friend asked the question and got a response. There is nothing abnormal about that. We would prefer not to have those experiences, but they do happen. For many, the expected answer "How are you doing?" is "Fine." The salutation is not an invitation to sit down and have a chat about where you are in the grief process. So do not feel that every person who inquires is requesting an in-depth, transparent response. In general, people want to be supportive but are not quite sure how to be. What sets helping individuals apart, the ones who desire to assist, is that they are frequently the ones who give you space to be yourself. They will call for a chat and in the conversation express their concern, and they will not walk away when the response may make them feel uncomfortable. Identify those who are helpful and allow them to be supportive. Trust is not something you give; trust is something people earn.

This information is not about keeping people away, never speaking of your grief, or implying that no one cares. Please know that not everyone is clueless about what you are experiencing. Some can be very helpful and supportive, especially those who have experienced similar loss. An indicator of what type of response is appropriate for the question is the setting in which the question is presented. If the setting is a public place where other people are gathered and the question is asked in passing, the question is simply a greeting. If the question arises in a private setting, then it is in your hands to determine how transparent you want to be and whether this individual is trustworthy enough to speak with. If someone is pushing himself or herself into your private space, digging for information about you and your family, do not share anything with him or her. Trust is earned, not given, and certainly not demanded, so in this situation, be guarded. For any question asked in a public setting, a generic response is all that should be given. I write this in response to particular question: "Does anyone really mean it when they ask how you are doing?" The answers is yes, but remember that if the setting is not a place to have a heart-to-heart conversation, then the question is a general, well-intended hello, and the appropriate response is, "I have good days and bad days. How are you and your family?"

Unit 33

Adjusting

The "adjusting" is becoming aware of the new normal, the feelings of wanting to kick, scream, cry, withdraw, be sad, not leave the house, not go home, keep to yourself—all along not wanting any of this to be true. Adjusting is crying in the shower because "no one will notice the tears" or screaming into the pillow because "I don't want people to hear me." You may think, *I don't want people to think I'm crazy because I act this way.* Perhaps some who are reading this wonder, *How does he know I do that?* Others may wonder, *What is he talking about? I don't scream into the pillow. I scream at the top of my voice while in the car.* Others may think, *None of that applies to me.* Well, this is grief. Everyone does it differently, yet there are similar experiences. Some take a walk in the woods. The separation that death brings is often greater than we could have ever imagined, lasts longer than expected, and causes us to feel things never felt before. There is no easy way to say that life goes on with or without the one we love. The value of life, your life, must never be underestimated, and the impact of death is often beyond words. Adjusting is dealing with everyday thoughts, actions, and schedules. A correct evaluation or assessment of life can only be done looking from eternity backward, not from today. It is from eternity that we see life's true impact. The difference a life makes, the difference of your life, is also unfolded each day as you interact with those you love and those who love you. Create good memories here in this moment when family and friends stop by to visit. Invest something of you in them each day. A smile is a good place to start—a smile that focuses on them. Even giving a hug is helpful; it is hard to give one without receiving one. The focus can be on letting others know that they bring something good into your life.

Unit 34

Mistakes in Grief

It is surprising how many people mistakenly feel that to grieve "properly" or "successfully" is to forget the person who has died, to become too busy to think, or to never mention his or her name, hoping these actions will push the deceased and all things associated with him or her to some remote place in the mind that is beyond access and beyond grieving. This is not grieving; this is denial. Grieving is not avoiding, eluding, ducking, dodging, denying, and disavowing a past relationship. The goal of grief is to remember and to embrace memories with love and sorrow, knowing that these memories are of such value that you made a life of them.

One individual who experienced the death of a parent at nine years of age spoke of her memories now that she is in her sixties. She remembered the times when she sat on her father's lap and read stories, remembering these times with fondness. When she was nine, her mother framed the grief experience with a mandate to forget about her father and informed the child at the time of her father's death that her father's name and position (father) would never be mentioned again. This child, who is now a physician, cried her first tears for her deceased parent in the last year. She had finally discovered that what was presented to her as a child was not the best way to grieve. Her mother's approach of never mentioning her father's name again was not done out of meanness or abuse. This disowning method was the mother's way of surviving. She knew only this response as her "normal" way to grieve. Many have sincere ideas regarding how grieving should be done, and they are sincerely wrong. The difficulty lies in understanding the purpose of grief. They must understand that tears and sorrow are not wrong and that memories are not forbidden. If you love someone and he or she dies, it will hurt and you will have memories. The goal is not forgetting. We cannot forget yesterday's experiences as if we had a magic eraser. Yesterday, good or bad, is part of who we are; it is all of our yesterdays that have brought us to this moment. Even if there were some not-so-good times in our lives, forgetting is impossible and pretending that the deceased did not exist becomes denial. The goal is to deal with hurt in a healing way and in manageable segments. (If there were abusive times or a painful past, let a professional help with these memories. It is important to remember but in a way that will heal the wound.)

Similarly, a person's dying does not make him or her a "saint." A common expression is "You can't talk ill of the dead." Every person and every relationship has difficult times. In grief, we feel guilty for our part in the difficult times, but we need to remember that it takes two to fall in love, to make it work, and to disagree. The "making it work" times are the ones when we disagree and yet love enough to stay together and see things through. Memory is not the enemy, but selective memory becomes a problem— when one chooses to view past experiences with a personal bias to prove someone wrong or something correct. Using selective memory to pile guilt upon oneself to the point that you cannot go on is not conducive to moving through the grieving process. Selective memory is choosing only certain events and taking them out of the context of time and place. Remember, you survived the event, so you can survive the memory. If you feel you need professional help, seek it. No one person has all the answers to every problem. Take the pressure off of yourself and allow someone to walk with you through this time of sorrow. The support conveyed in this section is intended to help unlock and unload the "out of sight" snags and the "left out of the story events." Do not carry these half-truths with you any longer. It takes more than a book to help expose such events and bring these painful places healing. Opening these locked-away areas to speak of them openly robs them of their power to control or to influence. Perhaps when these things happened, we hid them as a way of surviving the moment, which may have been the only way we knew to deal with them. Possibly we felt alone and isolated. Now is the time to rid ourselves of fear or guilt. It can be that fear and guilt guard this "no trespass" zone, but they will lose their power and influence if this protected zone comes open for discussion. Deal with it, disarm this danger zone, and speak what you know is true.

.

Unit 35

Returning to Work

Some consider grief a momentary crisis that will be neatly disposed of in a short period. Our society supports such concepts in its bereavement days allotted to workers. In a three- to five-day window, one can learn of a death, arrange a funeral, bury the deceased, and return to work. The concept of adjusting to the death of a child, spouse, sibling, parent, or any significant other in a few days is simply irrational. I become furious when I hear, "Take as long as you need, just so it is no longer than five days." It has the connotation of, "After all, how long will it take you to get back to normal?" Your workplace's policies control the number of bereavement days allocated. The allocation of bereavement days can also be made according to relationship: parents get you perhaps three days, while a spouse or child gets you five days. Other places have set bereavement times as three calendar days, which includes a weekend. With this time frame as a reference, grief would appear to be an adjustment that could be completed in a short time frame. If this were the case, normal life without the loved one should be only a few days or perhaps a few weeks away. As you are well aware, this is a flawed concept. To those who have experienced the death of a loved one such as an emotionally close family member or friend, five days is hardly long enough to find one's way out of the house. This limitation on grieving is based on an incorrect assumption.

In a support group, one person said that his boss warned, "If you cannot get your life together, the company will be forced to let you go." Another individual, just a few weeks after the death of her spouse, was informed of the need to lay someone off in her department; she was the one laid off because her productivity was down. (If this has happened to you, seek legal counsel.) Work environments can be supportive or cruel. Some welcome the return to work because the deceased was not part of the daily activity there. Some despise the work environment because of the indifference or even harassment of coworkers. The best and the worst people to work with are the ones who have experienced a death in their lives. The worst are the ones who have distanced themselves from the pain and its effect upon their lives. Now through your grief, death is reintroduced to their lives, and they want nothing to do with this mourning process. They can purposely try to restrict any form of grieving. This workplace grief can become complicated and be difficult to navigate. In your vulnerable moments, avoid confrontation; document your difficulties that may be presented at a later time as a grievance. Each work environment is unique; everything has changed for you, yet it appears nothing has changed. Be kind to yourself.

Unit 36

A "Trip Tick"

" What will happen now that my loved one is gone?" "What will life hold for me?" These questions arise repeatedly, spoken or unspoken, inferred throughout the grief process. Before, in what was normal life, asking one question and seeking an answer would be adequate. But in grief, the same questions continue but in different formats. The process moves through many months and even years. The experience of loss is as close as the memory with this question repeating itself. The answer to "What will the future hold?" varies depending on where you are in the grief process. Years ago, when our family traveled, we would get a "trip tick" from AAA, and they put together a page-by-page route. On this trip tick was information about the area, towns, cities, and region. My wife, ever the schoolteacher, would read the information on each page, offering the highlights of the region to the children. There was a continual update as the mile markers passed, assuring us that we were on the correct road and headed in the right direction. The challenge for grief is to understand information concerning grief in such a way that it helps each person feel secure as he or she travels the road leading through grief. This trip of grief is not one we choose to make, and the reminder of why we make the trip is ever before us: "My loved one has died. Now where does this 'trip tick' say that I am? Where do I go from here?" Our loved ones' deaths confirm the reason for the journey. The information given helps in determining what is in these areas we are passing through, but we find ourselves wishing that we had never started this trip. But there is no choice. We cannot go back in time. The task of grief is to discover where this road goes and what our surroundings are. This trip is different from other trips taken in life. We could be a day from the death of a loved one or two years from their death and question where this "trip tick" is going.

We all remember those anxious times traveling as a child or with children, wanting to know how long it would be until we arrived. "Are we there yet?" is the popular refrain. Of course, the question revolves around the child's concept of time. Even as adults, we become anxious about time, especially when we reason that there is a schedule to keep. In grief, healing the broken heart and recovering from the loss that death has brought takes time, and there is no sustainable schedule to keep.

You may have noticed that my way of illustrating is by using parables, or metaphors in the form of short stories or illustrations. These stories convey particular thoughts that relate something familiar to that which is unfamiliar. If some of the stories presented as illustrating a particular thought are unfamiliar to you and the connection is just not there, do not be anxious. It is just a thought, an idea. These illustrations are not top-secret keys used to unlock hidden areas of the grief process. The stories are illustrations that could possibly be helpful to some and not to others. If the stories become confusing, simply move on. Some sections may be easier for a woman to grasp, and some may be easier for a man. For instance, a person who has lived in rural Central America in a one-room hut and has never seen a two-story home will not grasp the idea of a home with many rooms or even floors. When I have visited rural El Salvador, I have seen an entire family living in one room. They have no concept of a two-story home with many rooms, running water, or an indoor bathroom. They have never seen these things. For many of us, the way people live in rural El Salvador is impossible to grasp. Stories and illustrations can make difficult concepts understandable, taking away the anxiety of dealing with the unfamiliar. One of my favorite connecting thoughts is linking the grief experience to the experience of a broken arm. This comparison presents a number of grief observations.

Unit 37

Broken Arm / Broken Heart

I imagine that all have seen a cast of some type on an arm or leg, or perhaps you have even had one of your own. A few things we know of a broken bone are that it is accompanied by a lot of pain and swelling, and it takes time to heal. If you have ever broken your arm, you know the pain; you personally know the experience of which I am speaking. The pain is a sure indicator that something has happened, that something is drastically wrong. The pain, although extreme, has a positive purpose—it will not allow you to overlook the fact that the arm bone is broken. The hurt of the break will not let you go on as if nothing has happened. The pain and suffering forces you to seek help. If there were no pain with a broken arm, many would simply act as if nothing serious were wrong and neglect to seek help.

The anguish experienced with the death of a loved one is just as real as that experienced with a broken bone. Never allow yourself to conclude that the death of a loved one is only an emotion that needs to be dismissed, as if nothing important has taken place. It is not true that if you do not pay attention to the pain, the break will heal on its own.

How do we get help for a broken heart? As many have experienced, finding help can be difficult, especially when so many individuals who connect to our lives have opinions about grief but may have little understanding of the grieving process. I never realized there were so many "experts"—people with an opinion about grief who give this judgment as sincere instruction. They have little knowledge as to what is involved in the grieving process but "know exactly" what you should do. These "experts" have no problem sharing their view of what is wrong with your life and how you should correct it. What marks this for failure is that these opinions are not backed by personal experience, only a judgment concerning what they would do if this ever happened to them. These individuals are the ones who have never been in water but believe they can teach you how to swim. They are full of senseless logic as they try to explain the skills and technique of swimming.

The pain associated with grief is difficult to comprehend. It is intensely challenging, especially at the beginning, when the certainty of loss can be relentless, unyielding, and often crushing. Along with this comes the questioning, "This cannot be normal, can it?" The bereaved may conceal their grief to make others think that everything is going fine. Society portrays grief as abnormal, as if grieving is to be keep a secret, those who are experiencing grief will not let others know how they are really doing because they stress over appearing inadequate. If you have to put on a performance to keep friends, they are not worth keeping. If performing is necessary to keep others from offering their senseless opinions, just walk away instead. With those who demand a routine of strength and say that "you need to listen" to their pressuring advice, simply let them know that you have your good days and bad days. Refuse to offer a display for critics to analyze. Some people do not need to know anything of your grief. The goal is not to hide or perform but to deal with what is going on in the moment in manageable segments, with a few (one or two) close friends or a counselor. Take time to be open with your thoughts, fears, and emotions but only with a select few and in safe places, not in a public forum. The people who are most likely to understand are the ones who have experienced similar loss and will not make a public production of their concern. Some people will be supportive, and some are just senseless. The clueless people suggest resolutions, telling you to sell your house, go on a cruise to meet someone, go out and party to get your mind off of this, get over it, do this or do that, move on, go back, or forget about it. These ideas do not bring comfort and are misguided.

With a severe arm fracture, your arm would be extremely sensitive even when placed in a cast, and no matter what you thought or tried, it would throb as if it would explode for the first few days or weeks. The pain of grief can feel as if your heart will explode. *Please* note that the trauma of grief is real, the stress of grief is real, and the pain you feel is real. If the pain in your chest, jaw, arm, or back is frightening to you; if it feels difficult to breathe; or if a physical symptom is different than what you have "normally" experienced or is unfamiliar pain, seek help. Go to your nearest emergency care facility and have it checked. It is better to err on the side of caution than to have an event that could be life threatening. There are similar physical indicators in grieving, as in physical body organ failure such as a heart attack, and *only* a doctor can tell the difference. Be safe and see a doctor. The pain of a broken arm would force a visit to an emergency room; likewise, the emotional stress of grief can create physical problems. Be safe with your life, and see your physician. Schedule regular checkups. Inform your physician of all the events that have happened in your life and how you are doing emotionally and physically, such as sleep patterns, eating, physical pains, hopeless thoughts, and so on.

Know when to walk away from senseless, well-intentioned advice givers, and know when to respond to good ideas. Our grandson, who is three, provided a good example when he was learning how to go potty. Bubba (his name for his grandma) was with him in the bathroom helping to get his stepstool in place, upon which he proudly stood with his pants down as he got ready to proceed with the much-anticipated potty training. Then, he turned and said, "Walk away, Bubba. Walk away." Great advice from a three-year-old! He knew when to seek help, and he knew when he had enough help, at which point he sent his grandma out of the bathroom. He could handle the next steps by himself. If only we all had the sense of a three-year-old.

A broken bone has a way of convincing you of the urgent need to do something immediately. The pain sends you to the emergency room to confirm what you already know. If a friend called and said, "I think I broke my arm," how would you respond? Most likely, you would inform him or her to seek help by going to the ER and having it examined. You would never say, "Put a bandage on it. The bone that is sticking out will heal on its own." How senseless! I cannot imagine someone giving such guidance, and if such advice *were* given, we would have enough resolve not to consider this a final solution. Senseless individuals always find an occasion to make their foolishness heard. It saddens me to remember statements made to bereaved people standing by a casket, such as, "You can always get married again," "You can have another child," or "You have other children." One I recently overheard was, "I am sure she is happier in heaven than she looks in the casket." These individuals are senseless and "stick a bandage on a broken bone" clueless, offering absurd thoughts as comfort. "Walk away, Bubba. Walk away." Do not listen to or give a second thought to senseless people. In this case, you walk away. These senseless people are like dogs howling at the moon. You cannot stop their actions. It is their natural thing to do.

When you arrive at the emergency room with a broken arm, the receptionist will take your name and information, and (I say this optimistically) upon seeing the severity of the fracture, escort you immediately to a room where the ER admission process is begun. A staff member or doctor will come to conduct an initial assessment and then send you out for an X-ray. The doctor will returns with a reading and a diagnosis: "You have a broken arm." *No kidding!* you think. *My arm is bent in ways it should never be, and this bone protruding through my skin is a definite sign that my arm is broken. I could have told you that! The pain is unbearable, and you had to do an X-ray to tell me that my arm is broken?* (Note that the frustration stems from wanting something done immediately to relieve the pain. When in pain, we are not our normal selves, even though we know that a procedure must be followed to assess the complete injury.) At that point, perhaps, the ER doctor will call in a specialist who is able to set broken bones. This specialist will come and take you to the operating room, where the compound fracture can be properly set. The purpose of the surgery and the cast or special apparatus used is to ensure that the bones are in alignment and set so that they will grow together. The goal is placing bones together in such a way that the break will heal properly. Of course, this is my version of a broken arm and visit to the emergency room. I was part of the hospital setting for thirty-three years, so I am knowledgeable enough to say that each situation will be different than I have just described. All have the same goal, just different ways of getting there, following different protocols. The same applies in grieving—the goal is the same, but there are different ways of getting there.

The pain of a loved one's death, grief, is just as real as the pain of a broken bone. The variables lie in that grief has no emergency room, grief has no X-ray or test to diagnose a broken heart, and there are no surgeons to perform emergency operations in "setting" this shattered experience. The only help there appears to be is words—words that are difficult to hear and understand—and touches and hugs from caring people, all of which embrace a numbness that is vaguely associated as "me."

Perhaps it was in an emergency room or a hospital setting where your loved one died. Maybe the news of your loved one's death was explained to you by hospital staff as they extended their sympathy and escorted you to the room where your loved one's body lay. Perhaps the staff encouraged you to take some time with the deceased. This time is an experience never forgotten; it is as close as your thoughts with accompanying visual reminders, feelings, and smells, as if it has just happened. Perhaps you were with your loved one as he or she took that last breath, experiencing shallow breathing and the extended time between each breath, apnea, until the final breath.

Grief is not like reading a book; it is a collection of experiences felt and memories recalled. For those who were by the side of a dying loved one, the desire to keep them from being alone was the goal. The experience is not without its memories. Perhaps it was a difficult death and the memories are ones we wish we could forget. It is a trade-off between being there and having memories. The comfort given by your presence is more important than what is remembered. I speak of these "deathbed" experiences to inform you that others who have been at the sides of their loved ones also struggle with remembering. You are not alone or abnormal. The death was shocking, even if it was expected; nothing prepares us for that moment. These memories are forever etched in our minds, although possibly pushed aside and not recalled until later. It is important to connect the emotions with the experience. They belong together. Nevertheless, no matter how our loved ones died or how long we spent with the deceased, there is a time to leave and return home. In that moment, life forever changes. Everything felt, said, or done has just ended. Future connections to our loved ones will be through memory. The exchange of words and touches will come second-hand through objects associated with your life together. What a sorrow-filled experience. The tears you shed are tears of sorrow for the one you love. They flow from a broken heart, and no matter how long it has been, remembering their loss and what they mean to you is important. We cannot live there at that moment, but for some, it may be the first time to revisit. Take time to be with your thoughts and express your heart. Write in your journal.

There are also deaths that take place when we leave the room for a few moments. I have been with families who have maintained a vigil at the bedside of a loved one, and then, for whatever reason, when all of the family is out if the room, the patient dies. Perhaps the patient just wanted to be alone; perhaps he or she did not want to put others through any more sorrow. Not being there comes with its own feelings of remorse. Beating oneself for not being there is not helpful. Some dying patients wait until a loved one arrives, while others die just before they arrive knowing all will be together. I believe the patient takes comfort in knowing a family member is coming, has arrived, or has been with him or her and leaves for a moment. How much control we have over the last breath is uncertain. We sometimes see patterns, but each dying person is different. Hollywood has depicted the "perfect death." The good people arrive just in time to say good-bye, and the patient takes his or her last breath and expires. A grieving actor places his or her hand over the eyes and gently closes the eyelids. Death has come, and the scene is over. In reality, dying may take hours or days, and after death, many will keep trying to close the eyelids or prop up the chin to close the mouth. Many remember that in "the old days," people would tie the mouth closed with a towel. *Should we do that now?* they may wonder. Real life is not like television or the "old days." Do not use a staged environment to compare with a death experience.

When death occurred, you may have "found it" ("it" being grief, not "lost it") with tears of sorrow, holding or laying with the deceased. This common phrase, "They lost it," is not misguided, as if tears are an expression of being out of control. Another phrase, "broke down," is equally inadequate, as if the expression of grief has caused one to stop functioning like a car that breaks down along the road. The bereaved now becomes something to fix, as if tears or other expressions are abnormal, as if one is wrecked. If your car breaks down, it stops running. Being responsive to the impact of death is a normal reaction to loss. To go on with life as if the deceased never existed—*that* would be a problem. Grief is a distinct personal expression. Do not complicate grief with daytime television or Hollywood flashes of sorrow, where actors portray unrealistic experiences.

With a loved one's death, the hospital staff needs to know what funeral home to contact before you leave. The reality of what has just happened takes time to filter through, but at this instant, the establishing of life without your loved one begins. The reality of what has just happened, death, may take a while to sink in as you say, "I can't believe this happened." It may take hours or days to filter through the surprise and disbelief. The mind can absorb only a defined quantity of trauma. Of course, each person is different, and that is cause for the varied time to grasp the actuality of death. Nothing can prepare you for this moment, even if you knew it was coming. In an instant, everything has changed. Even if the loved one had been ill for a long period and the funeral arranged for years, death comes as a shock. You are leaving the hospital in pain and wondering if this is a nightmare. The normal patient hospital experience is one of coming to the hospital in an emergency situation with anguish and pain, not leaving that way. Now the greatest emergency of life has occurred, and you are walking away. Grief is confusing. It is no wonder it makes you feel like life has turned upside down. Then, your belief system says that your loved one is in heaven, happy, but that has little or no effect at this moment. You are there—sad, shattered, and in disbelief. You are hurt, spiritually disappointed, emotionally devastated, and physically exhausted. Your heart is broken, dreams of a life together are crushed, and there is no cast for a broken heart, no surgery to repair the brokenness, no sling to hold your heart.

For a broken arm, the break is set, a cast is applied, instructions are given, precautions are conveyed, and a return visit is scheduled with a doctor. At that first appointment, the doctor may take another X-ray, ask how the arm is doing, and make another appointment for cast removal at the six- or eight-week point from the break. At the end of six or eight weeks, the doctor may do another X-ray to make sure the bone has healed properly, remove the cast, and prescribe some type of physical therapy to strengthen the arm. The healing process is not complete with the removal of the cast. Now starts another phase referred to as rehabilitation, which involves trying to regain strength and use. With a broken arm, the recovery time varies; it could take nine months, a year, or even longer for complete rehabilitation. Some persons have even said that they never regained full strength in their arms.

How long does it take to heal a heart shattered at the death of a loved one? With the death of a loved one, the "normal" hospital setting does not follow up with the bereaved to determine how well he or she is healing. The bereaved decides whether he or she needs help; otherwise, it is assumed that the heart will heal and the emotions will return to normal.

Does the phrase "stick a bandage on it" apply here? I do not imply that this is neglect on the part of hospitals or emergency rooms. They are in a reactive position, handling accidents, surgeries, and crises. Their service originates after a problem arises. In recent years, some facilities have become proactive in creating wellness programs that promote healthy lifestyles and exercise programs to keep people well. Such programs are available at certain facilities, but you must travel to them. In bereavement, it is assumed the that bereaved will seek help if they so desire. There are hospitals, hospice programs, funeral directors, counselors, therapists, and facilities that offer bereavement groups. The need is for the bereaved to seek them out.

General hospital professionals and even religious leaders are not trained in handling grief. The numbers of those who can help are increasing, but unfortunately many skipped that area of training. Grief creates a sense of "not knowing the right words to say" or "I do not want to say the wrong thing" or "I do not want to make them cry." For the bereaved to find support, it is their responsibility to seek help. The feeling for many bereaved is that death has brought some kind of disease that people want to avoid. Please know that others avoid grieving people not because they perceive a disease but because they are unsure what to say or do. Just the other day, I was in the hospital for physical therapy. A friend came and asked me what she should say to another friend whose adult child had died, adding, "I don't want to say the wrong thing." A counselor or therapist begins with a discussion about what you are experiencing or by saying, "Tell me what happened." Physicians often focus on what you are physically experiencing. People are comfortable with different roles, and many become uncomfortable when it comes to death and those who grieve. That is why you must be sure to explain to your physician that your loved one has died. Your doctor may not be aware of the death, and he or she may make a referral to aid with the needs you are experiencing.

I remember hearing someone say, "When I was falling in love, I didn't ask the doctor to check and make sure all was going well. All I wanted to know was if I was pregnant." Grief is different. When your doctor asks, "How are you doing?" be very straightforward with your answer. Completely describe your physical and emotional indicators. The sorrow of grief can mask physical problems. Allow your physician to conduct the examination and draw the conclusions. Visits to your doctor are very important, especially early in the grief process. Take care of yourself. Grieving is a difficult process physically, emotionally, and spiritually.

To those who have experienced both a broken arm and a broken heart, it is easier emotionally and physically to handle the broken arm. *I would suffer a thousand broken arms to have my loved one alive again!* you may think. The grieving experience will require a progression of time to be complete. Life will need special care for extended periods, as a cast and rehabilitation are required for a break. Grief is an up-and-down process, a roller-coaster of dips and turns, twists, and loops, and like the coaster ride, it can leave you staggering and dazed. A compound fracture requires a specialist who can perform surgery and align the bones. In grief, you may also need a specialist, one who deals in grief. This is not a sign of weakness but an indicator of the severity of the "fracture." The recovery time and rehabilitation for the arm cannot be rushed, nor is there a rush in grief recovery. The time needed to achieve the new normal, to figure out life without your loved one, is an extended time.

I once met a man who had a deformed arm and hand that rendered the hand unusable. I thought it was a birth defect, but when I inquired about what had happened, he said, "Oh, I broke it but did not have time to keep the cast on, so I took it off." His arm and hand had healed in such a way that they became twisted, deformed, and unusable for normal tasks. He had removed the cast because, at that place and time in his life, it was too restricting and got in the way. Allow time for your heart and life to heal. There is no rush. Remember, there are plenty of emotionally twisted people who felt that the healing time and effort required for grief was too long and too restrictive. Be kind to yourself. Healing takes time and effort.

A broken arm and a broken heart are similar but different. One is a physical break, while the other is emotional and relational. The pain experienced is similar but from a completely different perspective. In an X-ray, a radiologist can see a bone separation, a break. There are no separations to be seen in the muscle of the heart, but the physical death of a loved one, a person separated from your life, has occurred at death, producing the emotional and relational pain of loss and making the heart feel as if it is broken. The healing of an arm occurs faster and more predictably than the healing of the heart. Rehabilitation for the atrophy and diminished muscle of the arm from lack of use needs to be addressed if the arm is to return to its former strength, but the healing of the heart comes with the expression of love lost and with the expression of feelings, talking, sharing memories, and active living. Grief response can include going to familiar places, refusing to go to familiar places, remembering events of the past, trying to forget the past, creating new actions, creating new routines, keeping the old routines, sitting in the loved one's chair, or sitting across the room in your own chair while looking at the empty chair. Grieving is truly unique, just as loving is uniquely yours. Dealing with a loved one's death creates wounds to the emotions, feelings, and thoughts as if the heart in sorrow were broken.

Unit 38

Exempt Clause and Anger

The common "exempt clause" for grief expression is, "I express myself differently." This may be true. Each person is different, but the key is in "express myself." How is your grief expressed? A way to gauge whether there is grief expression—and not stuffed expression—is if there are anger problems. Not all anger issues result from a lack of expressing oneself for grief-related concerns. But, do you explode more easily than you did before the death or the loss? Do little things "set you off" or cause you to "blow up"? The emotions connected to the loss that are kept bottled up on the inside will find their way out, often in areas where anger appears to be appropriate. If someone cuts you off in traffic, disagrees with your opinion, spills his or her coffee in your lap, or makes you stand in line longer than you want, you may find yourself letting everyone know that they had better get this problem fixed. Anger is more "socially acceptable," "manly," and "tough" than sorrow, sadness, or tears. The pain felt at death is just as real as the pain felt with a broken bone. The question for those with the "tough it out" view is, Will the broken bone go unset and unseen by a doctor because you can tough it out? No one is exempt from loss or the intense feelings that accompany the death of a loved one. Anger is like an infection that will not heal. When anger becomes the norm, there often is a box of collected anger issues. Inside this box is a collection of our most volatile concerns, which will feed off of one another, justifying themselves as legitimate needs whose expression creates a relentless, escalating atmosphere of anger, pain, and fear. Anger is a response to something that has touched a sensitive area, exposing raw nerves and feelings. A state of continuous anger is a sign that the broken bone or broken heart is not set properly, and the "short fuse" comes from constant irritation.

We are aware that leaving a broken bone unset will lead to complications; likewise, leaving the emotional needs that accompany a loved one's death unattended will lead to complications. Sorrow and grief can be private expressions; some need their private space. But going on as if nothing happened is not grieving. Going off alone to think, to take a ride, or to walk down the street or in the woods to express the sorrow and the love missed is good thing. Grief will find its personal expression, but rage and fury are not healthy. Another image used for individuals who feel exempt from grief is a pressure cooker. The heat is on, the temperature on the inside of the sealed cooker is rising, the lid is locked in place, the vent for the steam is closed, and the pressure is rising. Sooner or later, the pressure cooker will explode. For those who have anger issues, the temperature is always hot, the pressure is high, and all it takes is one little thing to turn up the heat and cause them to blow up. The best way to handle the pressure in a pressure cooker is to turn off the heat, open the pressure valve, and lower the pressure on the inside. Sometimes, we just need to "blow off a little steam." But if doing so means displaying anger by hitting, pushing, screaming, engaging in road rage, belittling, calling names, intimidating others, and so on—all the while declaring that you have it all together—it is time to get help. Uncontrolled anger will turn to violence. Consider this: the anger problem began with not allowing the expression of sorrow over a loved one's death, an expression that was thought to be "out of control" or "out of character." In the final analysis, the devastation caused to one life by not grieving, by stuffing down emotions, has done more to damage than the natural grief response would have. Just as no two breaks are the same, no two emotional responses to death are not the same. The awareness that grief can last for an extended period allows us to the turn down of heat on the "pressure to be well." Seeking help from a knowledgeable source is an important option, as long as it is the kind of help that allows you the freedom to be yourself while disassembling barriers and turning off the heat.

Unit 39

The Funeral

You may be curious about why I placed this topic here instead of at the beginning. The funeral and perhaps the dinner following leave the bereaved to focus on getting things in order and what he or she will do next; there has been no time to review the events of the funeral. Or he or she is so consumed with the death and the grief that it is impossible to think. It is all overwhelming. The desire to review what happened at the funeral can arise a few days to a few months later. When the bereaved arrives at the confident, comfort emotional place where speaking of the funeral is something they wish to do, it is not regressing; in fact, it can be a way to put those events to rest. Discussing who was at the viewing and what was said can be a healthy journey. Others may have moved beyond this point and not want to go "backward" in their grief by speaking of or reviewing the events around the funeral. They may say things like, "That was a yesterday; let it be," or "It's over and done. Move on." Each family member has his or her personal relationship with the deceased, and that relationship determines the feeling of loss. A person dies—to one he was a spouse, to another he was a parent, another a sibling, another an adult child. Each of these individuals will have a different feeling of loss based on relationship to the deceased. Their thoughts on what to do or not do will come from those perspectives. To the spouse or parent, the grief can be so intense that everything that happened around the funeral is a blur; since things will be unclear for them, the bereaved may want to know what others remember of that time. It is okay to revisit.

The events surrounding the death and funeral are seen from different vantage points—adverse or positive. If you have an adverse viewpoint, you consider the cluster of people at the viewing and remember how much their attitudes changed as they moved through the line. They laughed and told stories of their lives, their families, and their jobs; *but*, you think, *my loved one will have no more stories to create.* You are left looking on from the outside, alone. The viewing is intended to be a time of support for you, but at times, it may feel like no one is really there; they all just come and go like shoppers at a checkout counter at the grocery store who pay their sorrowfulness and leave. It is all a blur. You could feel that it is your "duty" to stand vigil at the casket, forced to view the lifeless body and speak of the person there in the past tense, all the while thinking, *I can't stand to look at him. This is not real. It is all a nightmare, and I will soon awake.* The vigil becomes an endurance marathon of standing, greeting, talking, smiling, thanking, and wondering if this day will ever end. The rush of close family and friends moving in and out of line can be overwhelming. The "rescue patrol," or the ones from out of town, rush in, rush around, rush through, and rush back home. Their entire time at the house is spent helping, doing, and preparing, but they make you sit someplace "out of the way" as if you have suddenly become incapable of ordinary tasks. The viewing, the funeral service, and the meal are done, and then they are all gone. *I'm alone,* you think. *What the family and friends refused to allow yesterday is now happening, and they are gone. I am alone, doing today what I was incompetent for yesterday. I am alone to live life in this strange place that once was home. They have all gone. Can somebody tell me what just happened? The food in the refrigerator and the fact that things have been rearranged indicate that people were here. But why were they here? Has something terrible happened? There is no one here but me. Is it true that someone has died? Why should I clean up? I must go on. There are many things I must do for ...? I was told to be strong, but I have never felt so weak and so alone. My loved one has been away before; I can do this.* The thoughts come like fast-approaching storms, with wind, lightning, thunder, and downpours. Then there's a brief pause and another storm. "Can someone talk with me about the funeral?"

However, the funeral visitation provides many positives, such as receiving hugs, offering a time to honor the deceased, and sharing comfort from family and friends. The things that brought pain also bring support. The family recounts old stories and memories they shared with one another. All of this provides a distraction from the intense sorrow. Even the distraction of listening is a strengthening moment. It is difficult to imagine the number of people touched by a single life—the line of people seemed to never stop and new faces brought new thoughts, reminders of comforts when life was different, and memories that are forever sacred. *My heart is broken, but the hugs helped to hold the pieces together. My arms ache from hugging, my body hurts from standing, and my mind is numb with thinking of a reality I do not want to know. Life has forever changed, but my loved one meant so much to so many.* What makes the difference between adverse and positive is the connection between those who are hurting and the ones offering support. People probably will forget what has been said but will never forget how you or your loved one made them feel.

I often say that, in grief, everyone involved will be at different places in the grieving process. Some will feel that others do not care or did not love the deceased because of how they are "just going on with life as if nothing happened." Some may wonder, *Why would they try to keep what happened at the funeral from me? Was it that bad?* This is why some families have difficult times in relationships after a family member dies; they grieve differently and often in ways that the others do not see. If there have been previous clashes between family members, they will come back to the present. These conflicts are resurrected wearing different clothes, but they are the same issues that created friction in the past. Do not take the bait—this is not the time or place to try to resolve former difficulties. With heightened emotional events such as the death, viewing, and interment, this is a volatile time. Keep things as routine as possible and try to honor the wishes of the deceased. Most likely, as you're reading this, the ruckus has already transpired, and now the patchwork begins.

Sometimes there is the battle of "I loved them more than you. Can't you see how I am grieving?" I have attended funerals where a police officer was present to keep the family members in check. For the bereaved, reviewing what happened at the funeral is not a bad thing; it's not to place to assign blame but to find healing. It can be very helpful. But the family member who videotaped the viewing and the reaction of loved ones to the deceased as a documentary to be viewed later proved to be a bit too much for his family. Allowing for grief expression in its own time and in its own way is important, but so is considering the ideas and feelings of those close to you. It's good to review with others to remember how the life of your loved one was treasured by those who came and those who sent their condolences. These memories can be very helpful, especially if you were in a hospital, needed medication to sustain you, or were just going through the motions, basically in shock. Each person moves through grief at his or her own pace; the goal is to have each area of life open to review. Remember that no two individuals will see things the same way. Be supportive of one another. In the months that follow, know that one family member may experience grief a certain way and another may experience that same grief expression months later. Do not look for issues that create friction, but be open to what is happening in life now. Allow yourself and others to be where they are in the grief process, knowing that nothing in this grief experience is off limits. In remembering the past, there may only be a need for a new listener (counselor, doctor, or therapist). The relationship is personal, and the expression is distinctive. Each will deal with the loss in his or her own way.

Before one particular funeral, a spouse who suffered from heart problems became physically ill. The family took her to the hospital, and the physician prescribed medication to help calm her during the viewing and funeral. This was a good decision to protect the life of the surviving spouse, but the medication, while allowing her to be there, prevented her from remembering anything that happened. Many weeks after the funeral, she was upset because she could not remember anything about the viewing, the funeral service, who came, what was said, and so on. Wanting to remember is not a bad thing. In many situations, it is a good thing. The suggestion was to have the family sit down, review the guest register, speak of each person they saw, and recall what each said. It became a healthy bonding experience for them. It was a great way for the adult children and their mother to remember and share their stories with one another.

Unit 40

Do Our Loved Ones Miss Us?

In the Bible, the book of 2 Peter records, "Don't overlook the obvious here, friends. With God, one day is as good as a thousand years, a thousand years as a day" (2 Peter 3:8 MSG). In eternity, time does not exist. There will be no seconds, days, or years to tick away or to measure time. Time will be no more. Revelation 22:1–5 (MSG) says,

> Then the Angel showed me Water-of-Life River, crystal bright. It flowed from the Throne of God and the Lamb, right down the middle of the street. The Tree of Life was planted on each side of the River, producing twelve kinds of fruit, a ripe fruit each month. The leaves of the Tree are for healing the nations. Never again will anything be cursed. The Throne of God and of the Lamb is at the center. His servants will offer God service—worshiping, they'll look on his face, their foreheads mirroring God. *Never again will there be any night. No one will need lamplight or sunlight.* The shining of God, the Master, is all the light anyone needs. And they will rule with him age after age after age. (emphasis added)

In heaven there is a continuous "now" with God as the point of reference. *Does my loved one miss me as much as I miss them?* you may wonder. The perspective I think of is this: Have you ever been deeply engrossed in a project or a place and then suddenly realized that hours have passed? I think of heaven as being a place of meeting Jesus face to face, meeting loved ones who have died, and taking in the beauty of heaven, and then, in what feels like moments in heaven, we show up. It may have been twenty years on earth, but in eternal time, "a thousand years as a day" (2 Peter 3:8). I would not want my loved ones to be distracted from the glories of heaven. After all, Jesus is with them, and He is with me, watching over every step I take. At some point in the future, we will be together. They will greet us at heaven's gate. (Just a thought.)

Unit 41

The Puzzle

Life forces us to change and to make adjustments and adaptions to how life is lived. Think back on all the changes you have made in your lifetime. Some of them were made by choice, some were by chance, and some were mandatory, as if no selection were possible. Changes came and life continued, no matter how difficult the times were. Some believe life is a gamble and that we are playing the odds. Some believe we have no choice; it is all laid out before we are born. Still others believe that we choose our own destinies. What do you say? In the movie *Forrest Gump*, Forrest said, "Life is like a box of chocolates. You ever know what you're gonna get." It's like we are working on a puzzle—we have so many pieces, and only part of the puzzle is finished. The pieces we have will not complete a section until tomorrow's pieces arrive. The creation of tomorrow's pieces has not yet occurred. With today's portion in hand, we attempt to complete the picture of who we are at this moment. But no matter how hard we try, the pieces fan out into an incomplete picture we cannot recognize. Frustrated with the puzzle's missing pieces and the fact that some of what we have in hand appear not to fit anywhere, we figure that these cannot be parts of our puzzle. This questioning forces us to remember that our lives are not complete; death has created a vacancy, a loss, of what made yesterday's picture complete and meaningful. Remember that all pieces connect to others. Those of yesterday will connect to those of tomorrow. Can there be a divine "good" in today? Romans 8:28–29 says, "He knows us far better than we know ourselves ... and keeps us present before God. That's why we can be so sure that every detail in our lives of love for God is worked into something *good* (MSG, emphasis added). In today's pieces of the puzzle, our loved ones' influence is seen in every part. They are absent but not forgotten. They are in our hearts, absent from what is seen but forever alive in heaven. One day, when our puzzle is complete, we will see them again.

Tomorrow's pieces will not arrive until tomorrow. The picture before us is incomplete, and the chore continues as we determine how yesterday's pieces fit into today's and tomorrow's picture. The past will fit neatly with tomorrow's outcome, but what we need has not yet arrived and will not arrive until the future is attained. The difficulty with this puzzle is that every day is an incomplete section, part of an entire life but not finished. Some of the important pieces, even those for yesterday, have not arrived. With this limited, partially complete puzzle, we wonder about the past, speculate on the future, and long for a stable present. As we are aware that life has its missing pieces, this picture is completed in sections, and its future image is coming into view. One day the puzzle will be completed, but not today. So look at what you have, be at peace with where you are, and work with what is in your hands. Tomorrow will take care of itself. God is with you, and no matter where you go, God is piecing together your life, for He is God, you are His, and He is working good in your life. Life is not falling apart; life is fitting together.

Unit 42

Dealing

Dealing is being free to think of every part of life with no restrictions, no barriers, and no "off-limits" areas. If it is the past, it is open; life in the present is here before us, and the future is in our plans, although we do not know what that is. In dealing with the present—this moment that we consider now—the moments follow moments and become days, the days become weeks, and then months turn into years. Dealing is a way to connect moments. As discussed earlier, we can understand the healing process in comparison to a broken bone. We feel the progression in the arm as it begins to hurt less and regain strength, but what about the healing process of the broken heart? Healing takes time, and some will take longer than others. With the arm, the pain begins to decrease after a few days or, for some, weeks. But in grief, the emotional pain of separation just begins to settle in during this time. The grief experience becomes more intense, as if the pain is getting worse instead of better. The pain in the first days or week after surgery for a broken arm will lessen. In grief's first months or even year, we may continue to have difficulty believing that our loved ones are not returning. The difference is that, in grief, we question, *Will I ever recover from this death?* The downward slide in these months is the normal progression. I realize that feeling as if we are not as good as when we started does not feel like progression, but it is. These months following death bring with them the realization that our loved ones are not coming home, and this perplexing assessment is the lowest point in the grief process.

This is not a race or a comparison between grieving individuals as to who is further along, who is "better," or who is "worse." There will always be those concerned about whether they are as bad or as good as another is, as if grief were a competition. We become aware of others who are going through comparable experiences and the pressure to do this "grief thing" in a superior way or faster than another. Do not allow this intrusion. The problem with comparison in grief is in trying to determine something that cannot be measured. It is the inside healing that matters.

Unit 43

Visiting the Cemetery

P eople have many wide-ranging responses to visiting the grave site. Some bereaved never go back, some go back every day, and some return three times a day. Some take flowers and notes to leave at the headstone, and some have taken a newspaper and a chair so they can read to their loved ones. Others have taken blankets to lie over the ground as if to offer comfort. Some take lists of issues that were never resolved, read them to their loved ones, and then bury the lists at the grave. Some take love letters and read them aloud, while still others take balloons, tie notes to them, and release them heavenward.

Every relationship has good times and difficult times. No person is perfect, and no relationship is perfect. The covenant for the uniting of two lives where "two become one" is unity at a level never realized until death comes. Every person in a relationship that stayed together to this point understood the principle of commitment and that staying together through both good and bad times is what mattered. Some were greatly in love, and some shared only a name. In the paragraph above, many expressions of love and grief are listed, but perhaps yours is one that needs to be added. Remember, for those who visit the cemetery three times a day, these expressions are important for now. It does not mean they will continue to do so for the rest of their lives. A goal at some point in the future would be to visit the cemetery once a day or once a week. For the person who has not visited the cemetery since the funeral, the goal would be to visit once—perhaps not today, but someday. Visiting or not visiting has a personal significance that is particular to the bereaved. In time, that meaning will change, not because their love is any less but because that love will have a different expression. Visiting the cemetery is only one part of grief that has its particular expression. Looking at what keeps us away or what keeps us coming back is of personal importance. Know what barriers present themselves as reasons not to go or reasons to go three times a day. There is nothing wrong with either way. It is personal expression. Guilt is not a reason to go or to stay away. No guilt trips are permitted.

When you love someone and that person dies, how could you not miss him or her? Our expectation was to live a lifetime with them, and our lifetimes are still going on. The assumption that faith bypasses grief is a wrong concept and is wrongfully circulated. The faith that we possess does not cancel out our pain, and the pain does not cancel out our faith. When we use faith to feed denial, the comfort we seek will not come. Our emotional and mental makeup can allow only so much information into our thinking. The process of recognizing that our loved ones are not coming home can take time. These are safeguards to prevent overloads, burnouts, and disconnects in our mental and emotional circuits, like the circuit breakers that prevent short-circuits from plugging in too many appliances into an outlet. The circuit breaker is a safety switch to prevent overloads and electrical fires. This is a normal response for our mental and emotional systems. Buffers are the things we tell ourselves, such as that our loved ones are on a trip, in heaven, or at work. Faith also can be seen as a buffer to the reality or the impact of death. These thoughts help buffer the realities of a loved one's absence.

One day, some adult siblings requested that I speak with their mother. When the mother arrived, she began by telling me that her husband was having an affair and would not eat supper or come to bed. He would just sit in his chair until morning and then get up and go to work. The adult children interrupted the story and stated that their dad had been dead for ten years. They added that their mom had done so well when their dad had died. She believed he was in heaven, she was happy about that, and she went on with her normal life as if nothing had happened. Somewhere in her faith, denial had moved in. In the pressure to be well, things had become confused. The widow refused to speak of her husband's illness or death. She also refused to return for another session. I made a referral for the siblings and to the widow to at least see her primary physician. Going on with life as if the death of a spouse, a child, or a close friend did not happen creates problems, even if the deceased is in heaven. (Denial in the beginning of grief is a normal response; however, it becomes complicated when denial persists for an extended period of time.) When you love someone and that person dies, it will have an impact on your life. Grief expression is a normal response to loss.

Unit 44

Is It Okay to Laugh?

Did you ever think that laughing would create such a problem? In a group setting where all present had experienced the death of a loved one, someone would speak of a humorous experience and there would be spontaneous laughter. An individual would realize that he or she had been laughing and leave the group crying. Of course, we would speak with that person, bring him or her back to the group, and discuss what it felt like to laugh for the first time. Many expressed how traumatic it was, saying that laughter was not permitted and that it should not be part of the grieving experience. Some would say, "If you really love someone and they die, how could you ever be happy again?" or "If you are happy, does that mean you did not love them?" Some expressed that laughter or even feeling better was not permissible because it indicated that they were leaving their loved ones behind. This is another of those difficult places in the grief journey—when feeling better produces guilt. Some have called this a minefield of grief because no matter where you step, it blows up on you. If you feel good, you are guilty of not loving the one who died. If you feel lousy, you are guilty for not wanting to go on with life. The answer is in giving ourselves permission to cry and to remember *and* giving ourselves permission to laugh and to enjoy family and friends. Living encompasses a complete package of all emotions and all relations. Grief over time will give way to the other emotions not associated with sorrow. It is important that we give ourselves permission to be a complete person even though we feel incomplete. Learning to live again is learning to remember experiences in context and to experience all that life is now presenting. It does not mean that we take up skydiving for a hobby, but it can. We lived life before and found happiness; the life ahead of us can also hold happiness. Life will be good again, just not today. It is okay to laugh, it is okay to cry, it is okay to remember, and it is okay to dream. But in this moment, give yourself permission to be where you are and make the most of the life that is in your hands.

Unit 45

Fear and Safety

Fear can be a paralyzing experience. Perhaps you have heard the expression "deer in the headlights." If you have ever driven in the hills of Pennsylvania, you know exactly what the phrase means. It is a common experience to be driving there, especially in the fall of the year, and see deer standing in the middle of the road. When driving toward them, the lights from the car reflect in their eyes, and they stand there as if paralyzed, looking into the headlights and too frightened to move out of the way of the oncoming car. Fear has the effect of freezing them in a seemingly inescapable moment of time, frightened to the point that they are incapable of moving. Not only do deer experience this fear, but it is also a common experience with us. Fear brings this paralyzing uncertainty, except we *invite* fears into our lives—the entire family and distant relatives, apprehension, paranoia, anxiety, worry, nervousness, dread, phobias, fear of living, fear of dying, fear of going on, fear of staying. There are more. Did I tag enough? Have any or all of these come to visit? They will want to stay. There are endless scenarios for fear. Some of these cause us to freeze when we should run, and others cause us to run when nothing is there. Some of the fears are real, and some have little or no substance. They are manufactured by a deceptive reflection. So which ones are real, and which ones are imaginary? When life has been turned upside down and inside out with grief, it is hard to know what requires attention. Pause for a moment, take a deep breath, and do not run as if something fearful is approaching. Remember the saying "Don't just stand there—do something"? Well, in this case, "Don't just do something—stand there." With the grief experience and the accompanying loss, there can be any number of reasons to be anxious. Startled by oncoming life, we freeze in place, wanting nothing to change, or we run from everything.

Some fears can be helpful; they may be indications that we need to pay attention to needs that exist in our lives. Fears originate either in our imaginations or in fact. With the deer that looks into the headlights of an oncoming car and does not know to move, it is scared, but a vehicle is fast approaching. Something needs to happen—the deer needs to move or the car needs to stop. That is a very real fear. An action is required: move, stop, or else. Then we have fears that have little substance. I refer to them as multiple-part fears. There is an element of truth to them, but most of the fear is false. The difficulty lies in recognize what is real and what is false or assumed. Fears have an origin in something. It could be an event or a perceived event, and what follows is so paralyzing that it feels as if it is chained to a place. I once heard a saying—I am not aware of its origin— that stuck with me: "Error always rides the back of truth." In this case, fear will ride the back of something real. If the fear had no basis in reality, we would simply dismiss the thought. Zig Ziglar said, "Fear is False Evidence Appearing Real." We are not to hide from fears but face them head on; we need to look beyond the light to determine whether it is an oncoming car or the light of a flashlight. Both are real, but only one is a danger; the other is someone coming to help. Face and understand fear. If you are uncertain, get off the road, find a safe place, and wait for the light to arrive. It will then be easy to differentiate which light it is. The best way to deal with fears is to face them and always get up one more time than you get knocked down.

Unit 46

Fear and Faith

W hat follows is a faith discussion to dismantle fear and to clarify the control that fear seeks to project over life. The Scripture in 1 John 4:17–18 says,

> God is love. When we take up permanent residence in a life of love, we live in God and God lives in us. This way, love has the run of the house, becomes at home and mature in us, so that we're free of worry on Judgment Day—our standing in the world is identical with Christ's. *There is no room in love for fear. Well-formed love banishes fear. Since fear is crippling, a fearful life—fear of death, fear of judgment—is one not yet fully formed in love.* (MSG, emphasis added)

A place where you understand God's love is a place where fear loses its influence. Love and peace equate to power and strength. Now, if we stand in the middle of a highway and are afraid of being hit, that is a good fear. Move away from danger and get off the road. Some have stated that faith will stop the car, but I move in the direction that faith will cause you to move off the road. A normal, everyday life with the goings and comings in life is one not lived in fear. The self-limiting fear that makes you ask, "Oh my, what am I going to do now?" is ones that makes you run from an approaching flashlight. This type of fear originates from perception; perhaps situations have occurred previously that bring out a predetermined, anxious expectation that anything that can go wrong will go wrong—an overreactive fear response.

You may also experience fear about your life changing. Perhaps your loved one's character was one of dependability and reliability. Perhaps he or she was a person whose physical presence brought security. Now, that area of life is vacant, and fear wants to move in. Fear has its own agenda, its own plan, for paralyzing, alarming, belittling, stressing, and worrying over ideas with thoughts such as, *I've never done this before.* The truth is, you may never have accomplished something prior to now, but that does not mean the task cannot be done, that you cannot do the task, or that you cannot supervise the task. The fear agenda describes the setting as hopeless and you as helpless, unable to take on what lies ahead. Fear proclaims doubt, leading a campaign against personal development. Fear arrives daily dressed in different garments of anxiety, worry, panic, stress, or bad pizza. Whatever fits the day or the mood or whatever name brings fright to you, fear will work to blind you with whatever your imagination can produce. Enter faith and love, which equal power and peace and identify that God is with us. His presence establishes peace, and in the middle of peace, we dismantle fear.

The story that brought the awareness of fear to this writing is a recent experience of someone who spoke with me about awakening in the night terrified. The story this person shared with me brought up occasions of others who had experienced fear as they were going through loss. Managing fear is finding the truth about what fear is using to make things feel as if they are out of control. Ultimately, God's love is the deciding factor when it comes to displacing fear. It is in this place of security where God keeps insecurity at a distance. Know that God's love holds our hearts, heals our wounds, and gives us strength for today and tomorrow. When God's love fills our lives, there is no place left for fear to inhabit. Fear is not a necessary component in grief, but it does approach our paths with its blinding light, hoping for the element of surprise. Remember the saying, "If the shoe fits, wear it." In this case, if the shoe does not fit, do not try to find your size. If fear is not part of your life, do not go looking for it.

Finding the correct question concerning the creation of anxiety is a good place to start. Begin with personal, relevant questions: Will I need to be concerned about money? How will the bills be paid? Who will put gas in my car? Who will mow the lawn? Who will prepare meals? Who will go to the store? How can I face people? They all want to know how I am doing. Every anxious moment has a start somewhere. Discovering the starting point is hard, such as, "My husband always put gas in the car. Now who will do it? He was my protector and my provider." Some have discovered that they do not want to learn how to put gas in the car. "It's not fair. (Now the fear.) The more I do on my own, the further I move away from the place of security I once had. (Another fear) If I become more independent, will it mean I did not love him?" There are many ways that anxiety or fear connects to routine things once done by a loved one. The answer is found as we speak completely of what the fear represents. This is the rest of the story. Neutralize the fear by facing it and challenging it. Allow someone to show you how to fill the gas tank. If you learn and still do not want to do it, don't. The decision is made to allow someone else to take on this job, and it is a decision arrived at by personal preference. In preparing a meal, speak about the fear in full detail and then decide to learn how to cook or to eat out. This is not a life-or-death decision; it is a decision based on preference. One person I know never does put gas in her car. She does not want to know how, so she decided to have her gas pumped at a full-service gas station where she also has all of the maintenance done on her car. There is a solution. We just need to find it.

Fear will declare that there is no solution, but faith and love look for solutions. There may be just one answer or a combination of many. The need is to identify fear for what it is, a paralyzer. Fear will have us sit facing a corner and declaring there is no way out. From where you sit looking into a corner, fear is correct. But faith and love have you stand and look around the room to discover that there may be multiple exits from which to choose. Fear's next step is to say, *You do not know what's outside that door.* With each decision made, fear tries to stop the progression. You may not know what is on the other side of that door, but the door needs to be opened, and then you can make another decision. In the search for a solution, we can catch many ideas in our resolve to do something. Making decisions that are 100 percent perfect is impossible. No one is perfect. However, failure is not final. It is a learning experience. Again, success is getting up one more time than you fall down. Only time and effort can determine what is to be called "failure," but from the future looking back, we may be able to tell that it was this occasion that led to future success.

Remember, "Error always rides the back of truth." In this case, if there were no element of truth, fear would not have a platform to present itself. The light of truth is in your hand, and you are shining the light of truth onto the darkness of uncertainty. Life is to be dominated with love and faith that God is with us, and as His children, nothing is impossible for us. The realities of life continue to build on the realities of God's Word, where we are solution-oriented, faith centered, love motivated, and hope empowered. We are a part of the answer to every prayer we pray. (I read that somewhere.) God has faith in us. I see the hope I possess as a reflection of God's faith in me and God's purpose for my life. Hope is certainty that God is active in our lives and that we will make it through this adversity. Faith in God and His love is the answer to displacing fear. Divine peace is divine power. The love of God brings security. His love displaces fear. As you fill a cup with water, the water moves the air out of the glass; likewise, love dislodges fear from life. Fill us with your love, Lord.

Unit 47

Belief and God

The unwanted experience of death has, from time to time, raised the appeal that there can be no God. It is not a question of faith gone missing but in people's hurting so deeply that they reasons that if God were involved, they definitely would not hurt like this and their loved ones would not have died. Belief does not cancel the pain of death, and pain does not cancel out belief. If belief were the cure for grief, all believers could go on with lives after a death as if nothing had happened. Imagine the love of your life leaving life as we know it, and you never missing them and going on living as if he or she had never been a valued part of life. That would be a great tragedy. The mistake discovered in grief, the mistake assumed to be part of believing in God, is that our loved ones are declared to be living on in heaven and that we should therefore have no sorrow. Grieving is not a mistake or a lack of faith. Grief declares that we miss them here, now, in earthly life. That is not selfishness. Grieving is not selfish! (I hear people say this, and it annoys me. Is love selfish? No. Love is finding the one who loves me for who I am, faults and all. Love is not selfish, and neither is grief.) Grief is a fact of life, one that Jesus experienced at the tomb of Lazarus as evidenced by the verse, "He wept." (John 11:35) The incorrect thinking is that the bereaved should not respond to the feelings of death, but it is impossible not to respond to a loved one's death and absence from our lives. Grieving over death and the separation that it brings cannot be bypassed or erased as if the loved one had never lived or loved. Eternal life is not the antidote or a vaccine for grieving. The Bible states,

> And regarding the question, friends, that has come up about what happens to those already dead and buried, we don't want you in the dark any longer. First off, you must not carry on over them like people who have nothing to look forward to, as if the grave were the last word. Since Jesus died and broke loose from the grave, God will most certainly bring back to life those who died in Jesus. (1 Thessalonians 4:13–14 MSG)

Pain, sorrow, and expressions of grief are not signals that faith is lacking. The expression of belief is intertwined with the sorrow of death. This interlacing or interlocking is like what takes place when you bring your hands together, lacing your fingers to make one hand. Grief and belief are not two separate fists fighting the shadow of death. The two hands are clasped, belief and sorrow, forming one hand. There are many misunderstandings of grief and faith. As the reference we just read says, "you must not carry on over them like people who have nothing to look forward to, as if the grave were the last word." We have a very real loss, and we have a very real faith. Both come together in expressing hope of eternal life for our loved ones and in expressing our sorrow over their absence from our lives. We believe that grief and faith find expression in the Scriptures and in our lives.

Once, when flipping through the television channels, a speaker got my attention, so I paused to listen. He referred to grief as a lack of faith and said that grieving was not for believers. I listened for a while, hoping that this statement was only an attention grabber and that he would explain the purpose of such a declaration. The explanation never came. He went on to build his misconception of grief. This well-intended but misguided message had little contextual Biblical truth. It was backed by no actual life experience of sitting beside someone who was dying or of walking with someone through the grieving process. The bubble of television ministry had swept grief into a make-believe cauldron of shallow faith and self-indulgent sorrow. I was saddened to think of how these ideas would affect those who were listening. This half hour of misinformation would create confusion and complicate the grief experience for Christians who were already wounded by loss.

Do not think that what is written in these pages is all there is to understanding grief. The information shared is like a great meal on a table with foods of all sorts. You could not eat it all nor could you try everything. But you try what is appealing, what fits your person. You take what is interesting, and even some of that will be discarded. Taste what's offered, and if it is not to your need or liking, set it aside. There is only one person who has all the answers; His name is Jesus. The rest of us are students.

Unit 48

Prayer

P rayer is a personal conversation between you and God. Differing from ideas where the emphasis of prayer is informing God concerning present events along with guidelines as to exactly how He ought to carry out the detailed instructions, prayer is to be a personal conversation in which we speak and also listen. The speaking is reflective of the close association that we have with God and that God has with us, in which we are transparent, open, and expectant, offering a release of open-handed appeal of that which is difficult or painful to our lives as if we were explaining for the first time our concerns to our counselor and friend. We recognize that God is all-knowing, or omniscient, so the information shared is specific in nature and liberating for us, as if we are conveying, or consenting to the need we possess to transfer it to God. This prayer of presenting and letting go is for our benefit. It is our statement of faith, believing that God will receive this request and respond.

Listening for God to speak does not involve the Moses dynamic, where this audible voice states commands or the finger of God writes on stone tablets. We are listening for His counsel. The relationship with God develops an understanding of what God values and defines what is important in life. Hearing God is recognizing how God incorporates His Word, the Scriptures, into our thoughts and prayers, and paying attention to distinguish our thoughts from His. God's response can take shape as a distinct impression upon our minds or through reading the Bible, a devotional, a friend, a song, a doctor, or even a new thought, but ultimately it becomes a reflection of His Word to our spirit. It is where our spirits feel connected to the Holy Spirit; it just fits. He brings peace.

As we read the Scriptures, we find interventions where God demonstrates the omnipotent ability to interpose an outcome that replaces an existing one (i.e., the healing of a blind man by giving him sight, calming the troubled sea, or feeding the five thousand from a few loaves and a few fish) Our conversation, prayer, is an indication of faith looking for this other outcome, this other path as an alternative way, one that does not include suffering or death. Accordingly, our prayer is constructed from our perspective as in creating an alternative. We pray, wanting to avoid pain, suffering, and death. We could do nothing less than to make such a request; we pray for another way. We know God has accomplished such actions, but also know that God may have another way. Even Jesus in the garden prior to the crucifixion prayed.

> **Then Jesus went with them to a garden called Gethsemane and told his disciples, "Stay here while I go over there and pray." Taking along Peter and the two sons of Zebedee, he plunged into an agonizing sorrow. Then he said, "This sorrow is crushing my life out. Stay here and keep vigil with me." Going a little ahead, he fell on his face, praying, "My Father, if there is any way, get me out of this. But please, not what I want. You, what do *you* want?" (Matthew 26:36–39 MSG)**

The difficulty of faith lies in knowing that God can intervene and has intervened, but in this present time He appears not to. If you are one of us who have prayed for wellness for a loved one who then died, this is a perplexing, painful, hurtful, and even angry time of questioning and disbelief. The answer lies somewhere between the "will of God" and personal faith to move the hand of God. These are normal feelings and thoughts. We find difficulty in interpreting the times and seasons of life and certainly this season that brought death. There will be a day of disclosure at some point in the future when we will all understand, but it is not today. We seek resolution; we seek the answers to the "why things happen as they do" questions. This seeking often falls short of understanding but not short of God's peace and love.

Prayer expresses the relationship that we have with God and that God has with us. God values who we are above what we do. His love and His friendship surround us constantly; He is never unsettled, He never wavers, and He never changes, regardless of our thoughts and actions. When you pray, look for the reflection of God's Word in the words of your prayer. The words you utter to God—some spoken but many unspoken—reflect your personal perception and personal understanding of the Scriptures. Prayer is not seeking collaboration with God as if making a promise to God that we will honor if He will answer our request. *Collaborate* means "to work with another person or group in order to achieve or do something" (Merriam-Webster Internet 2014). Prayer is not collaborating with God to achieve wellness or healing or to find a better way; it's not making a deal that if you do this, God is obligated to do that. When we direct these bargains to God, it is little more than trying to manipulate the predicted outcome. The chance of getting an answer to a prayerful bargain is slim. The hand of God is not moved with a bargain, as if we could offer God something He needs. The hand of God is moved by faith, not in the value of what is offered. If I have enough faith, can I change the mind of God? No. But if I have enough faith, I will know the mind of God.

The greatest needs in life are personal forgiveness with God and eternal life in heaven. All other needs fall below this primary objective—knowing God through Jesus Christ. What would we profit if we would gain the world and lose our souls? (Matt. 16:26). The reality is that God is offering us something we need, forgiveness, and the offer centers on His love, His grace, and His mercy. I know of those moments experienced while waiting helplessly at the side of a dying loved one; a passionate searching of the soul takes place in the midst of the desperation of clinging to life, offering a bargain with God, making promises, and pulling on every possibility to give life another chance. Please note that in the turmoil of the soul, the breaking of the heart, and the unbelievable pain of seeing our loved one die, we will try anything to give them life. "God, take my life, and let my loved one live!" we plead. There is nothing more that love could offer—our lives for theirs. God has already made that sacrifice, His life for ours. It is their time to go home.

With the certainty of prayer unanswered, we come to the misunderstanding that our bargain was not good enough, that prayer does not work, or that God has favorites and we are not among them. We know that prayer is more than informing God as to how we want life to work. Prayer is a conversation with God around the relationship that we have or expect to have, reflecting the Scriptures in our requests, and listening for the gentle expression of His presence by way of the Holy Spirit. The appearance of God's will is always in harmony with His Word. God, we do not understand, but we trust you.

Confusion of belief occurs when one prayer has an answer and another appears unanswered. One such situation took place in Scripture when Paul and Silas were in prison (Acts 16:16–34). They sing and pray, the earthquake comes, prison doors open, and they are free. (There is more to the story; take some time to read it.) The second situation is when Paul is in prison in 2 Timothy. There, Paul speaks of the greatness of God's mercy and writes letters to different churches. He states that he longs to see the different people but is unable to because he is in prison. Here is the question: Did Paul forget how to sing? Had he lost some quantity of faith? The first time he prays, an earthquake strikes and the prison opens, but now he remains locked up. No, it was a different season or time of his life. God was ministering through Paul in a different way during this imprisonment than in the first. He had now reached the conclusion of his ministry; it was Paul's time to come home to heaven. Could God cause another earthquake and set Paul free? Yes, but that was appropriate for a previous time in another season.

Many years passed between these two events, and Paul had experienced numerous miraculous events, as well as many life-altering and life-directing situations. If anything had emerged, Paul's faith to stay in prison was greater than his deliverance from prison. Was the Apostle Paul's life out of control? No. As you read 2 Timothy, where Paul's life and his impending death are spoken of, you can see that Paul is at peace with the coming events; everything is as it should be. He says, "I have fought the good fight, I have finished the race, I have kept the faith" (2 Timothy 4:7 New King James Version, NKJV). We see God working through Paul in each season of his life in different ways, accomplishing even more than is reflected in the written record. The faith that opened the doors to the first prison is the same faith that secured Paul in the last prison.

We cannot measure faith by what surrounds us or where we find ourselves. Faith withstands in spite of the circumstances; faith knows that God is with us and that His presence can never leave. Words can hardly express the greatness of hope that a few moments in the presence of God bring. It is in His presence that we come to know that life is not out of control and that God is with us. Knowledge will direct the mind, but His divine presence holds the heart. Knowledge and Spirit come together, bringing the understanding that God is with us. The awareness of the answer to our ultimate prayer arises. God is with us, our loved ones are with God, and we will see them again.

Unit 49

Trust and God

Trust and *God* are two words that belong together. When trust is wrapped in a package of "God, do as I ask," this is not trust but an ultimatum. God, who is all-knowing, has not broken our trust by not doing as told. Trust in God is reflected in outcomes beyond what we experience or could imagine. When in prayer, we make choices; we choose a direction with the knowledge and understanding that we possess. Life brings the awareness that we are not in control of events. We are in control of only how we respond to the events. Belief turns to a loving, caring heavenly Father who is the creator and giver of life, and our belief then carries us beyond the threshold we call death to the living God, with whom those we call dead are still alive. They are in His presence—our trusted outcome. Death appears to rob us of the life that we loved, but death cannot end life. Life is a gift from God, and life continues in the presence of God. Death cannot extinguish life; death does not have the power to snuff life out. God is with us giving us hope; the hope He gives is in His Word and through His presence. We are always safe in His presence.

It is difficult to solve the mystery of prayer and of why God does or does not answer requests as spoken in a few moments or words. We know that life is more than a segment of time represented by two dates on a cemetery headstone. We know that God is a relational being who desires to be part of our everyday lives, not just part of that ending date on the grave marker. God is not a magician who performs magic when called upon; He does not mechanically jump from a box when we turn the handle of prayer. God is not a spare tire allocated to the trunk of life to be removed only when life runs flat. The Bible is not a box labeled, "In case of emergency, pull this verse."

I find great comfort in knowing that I am safe in the arms of my heavenly Father, and from this place of comfort, security, and love, I deal with life. Our prayers and our relationships with God reflect each other. Just as a mirror reflects, so prayer reflects the relationship with God and His relationship with us. In this closeness of relationship, oneness is realized—oneness that will last for eternity. Nothing of this life will interrupt this relationship, not even death.

Prayer, then, is an expression of what I see and understand of God and His promises as expressed in Scripture. I speak these God promises in my prayers to God not to remind God of them but to remind myself of how limitless God is. In His limitless power and knowledge, I live my life knowing that nothing can ever come between us. His love is greater than I can imagine, His grace is beyond measure, and his power has no restrictions. He gives assurance to all of His children. God will never initiate any action in all of eternity to distance Himself from us. I pray and believe that nothing is impossible with God, and in this belief, I trust God to accomplish His purpose in the seasons of my life and in the lives of those for whom I pray. We know that physical life is fragile and that all human life will end at some point. Apostle Paul states,

Do you think anyone is going to be able to drive a wedge between us and Christ's love for us? There is no way! Not trouble, not hard times, not hatred, not hunger, not homelessness, not bullying threats, not backstabbing, not even the worst sins listed in Scripture: ... None of this fazes us because Jesus loves us. I'm absolutely convinced that nothing—nothing living or dead, angelic or demonic, today or tomorrow, high or low, thinkable or unthinkable—absolutely *nothing* can get between us and God's love *because of the way that Jesus our Master has embraced us.* (Romans 8:35–39 MSG, emphasis added)

Unit 50

Going Back to Church

Going back to church after the death of a loved one can be difficult for many reasons. We are reminded of the death and of our loss. There is a seat where we have always sat, and one person is missing. Continual reminders will be aroused by favorite music of love, of life, and of heaven. Then, the well-intentioned friends approach with "How are you doing?" and the extra conversations that speak of their assessments of how this could have happened and your grief response. It is sad when churchgoers do not recognize the impact of death and loss. Because of their lack of understanding of what is appropriate and inappropriate to do or say, they muddle their way through, hoping for the best. Those who know least what to say and do will make bold declarations, such as, "You know he is better off in heaven," "We cannot question God's will," or "You have other children." The desire to help is misled by absolutes that they think will solve the mystery or misery of grief. (This not only applies to church but any social group of which one is a part.)

Why do we cry in church? Our faith is more than just an intellectual assent; it is an understanding of God. Our faith is a foundation for this relationship. It is personal. It touches our emotions as well as our intellect. It touches our souls and our hearts. The tears we shed in church are tears of love, sorrow, comfort, and connection with God. If you had a cut on your arm, it would bleed. Likewise, tears flow from a broken heart. It is as natural to shed tears when you're sad as it is to bleed when you're cut. This searching area of our souls longs for wholeness, and it is often in God's presence that we shed tears and find comfort. One suggestion to consider is to visit church when no one is there and sit, walk, cry, and speak with God. If someone questions your tears in church, simply say, "Is there a better place to express my sorrow?" God and his love are touching this broken area of life. It is the Holy Spirit—God—coming together with the pain of our loss, bringing comfort and healing. So why do we cry in church? I feel that it is the result of God's touching our lives in a very compassionate way. We may never hear His voice, but we feel His divine presence. It is God letting us know that we are not alone in this grief. He is there with us every step of the way. He weeps with us, comforting those who mourn.

> The Spirit of God, the Master, is on me because God anointed me. He sent me to preach good news to the poor, *heal the heartbroken,* announce freedom to all captives, pardon all prisoners. God sent me to announce the year of his grace—a celebration of God's destruction of our enemies—*and to comfort all who mourn, to care for the needs of all who mourn* in Zion, give them bouquets of roses instead of ashes, *messages of joy instead of news of doom.* (Isaiah 61:1–7, emphasis added)

The place we most associate with God is in our church or a "sacred" place where we pray or walk.

Should we attend church? The answer is yes. Should we continue to be members of local organizations? Yes. To leave a familiar place creates another loss, but as with any reason to change, it has its perception in hurt, pain, and grief: "If I do not go there, I will not cry or bring up my sorrow." Familiar places have their own specific losses. It is in these places that we feel more vulnerable and where friends or acquaintances feel at liberty to say what they think, which can be hurtful recommendations. As we are experiencing grief, we ask ourselves the question, *Is the hurt intentional?* Forrest Gump said, "Stupid is as stupid does." Some people do not know that what they say is stupid and hurtful. Balance your hesitance to go with questions like, "Is there comfort in this place?" "Are there compassionate, supportive people there?" "Are there understanding people who identify with me?" "Are the pastor and leaders accepting of who I am and where I am in the grief process, or are there expectations for me to be over my grief because I am creating a barrier to their celebration?"

A young widow attended a social group with six other couples. After her husband died, they tried to welcome her back, but she did not fit into the couple setting as before. She had to find another group that was not made up of couples. Was this a bad group? No, but her needs were different than they were before. Things change, not out of malice but because life changes. It doesn't feel like what you need has changed, but it has. One place we see that change is in the get-togethers we attend. Sometimes what "was" does not fit what "is" any longer; this simply means that it is time to seek something that does fit—other friends and groups. Some changes are made by adding to the routine, some are made by subtracting from the routine, or some are made by just starting new routines. It depends on what works for you. However, what works in one segment of grief, such as during the first six months, may not work at the twelve-month point. Be open to where you are at this moment in dealing with events, memories, holidays, and groups. All this will change. Do not burn the bridges to your previous life before the death. Everything changes. You will go through the waves of grief, waves that push you forward, backward, up, and down and even roll you up. In this ocean, we long for the security of sand beneath our feet. When did we ever believe that standing in sand would be referred to as a secure feeling?

Unit 51

Love

We have all heard of love and perhaps have even had a personal experience with it. We have seen love expressed in many ways. We love many things—a person, a pet, a car, a house, an article of clothing, the day, a vacation, a day off, and so on. We love in different ways and for countless reasons. If we have love of the highest quality, it reaches a level of self-sacrifice. In this realm, love goes far beyond an emotion to an action, a behavior, and a changed lifestyle that reaches the magnitude of "willing to die for." This quality of love marks the pinnacle of what love encompasses. This level of love, compassion, and intimacy occupies every aspect of who we are. This love blends with every part of our being. When you love someone to this degree and the loved one dies, the emotional loss touches every distinct portion of your life. Every fragment of your being experiences grief. That is why grief comes in such a forceful way, creating a tsunami affect over your life. This love is the source of grief; it arrives with such demanding force that it overwhelms every part of your being. Each area of your persona where love is experienced—all that you were willing to sacrifice for the love of your life—now experiences vacancy and emptiness. And you feel the wound of loss. That's why we grieve.

Working through this vacancy of a loved one's death is grief. This grieving will take time and work. Rational thinking underestimates the emotional impact that death brings. Logic tries to make life black and white, life and death. *They were here, now they are gone. Now, go on.* Well, this does not work in real life. This thinking fosters the logic that one event brought pain, so another event should take it away. Some search for that one thing, one truth, one statement, or one thought that will cause the pain to cease. But there is no one things that can reverse the effect of loss. Nothing can mysteriously or magically dissolve grief. This is where individuals who seek replacements justify their thinking that since their spouses died, bringing in another will cause the pain to cease. Other people make themselves very busy, running from the pain and leaving no time for memory, but these only put off the healing of grief. People who avoid all thoughts of sorrow specialize in replacing. Being open with our losses, the impact they create, and the sorrow we experience is normal and a "healthy" part of grief. Grief becomes an everyday process of thinking, talking, feeling, doing, and journaling.

III. Section Three

Somewhere Between What Was and What Will Be

Unit 52

Why?

The *why* questions come in many different forms and at different times. The initial *why* questions can be *Why me? Why now?* and *Why this time of my life?* The other focus of *why* questions emphasize the deceased's life and lead to laments such as, "I cannot make sense of why someone so young had to die," "He did not deserve this," "She had so much potential," "He was doing so well," "She had accomplished so much and was going to retire," "Why would this happened to him and to this family?" "Was it in the stars, the will of God, the work of the universe?" "Was it fate?" The catch-all *why* question is, "Why do things happen the way they do?" My straightforward response: "I do not know." It is never wrong to question. *Why* questions about death seek meanings beyond life's discernment. We seek meaning that will give purpose to a death and help lessen the sorrow. But very few answers can decrease grief's intensity or bring a feeling that a death was purposeful. Knowledge is helpful in bringing balance or stability to grieving but not an end.

I think of a tightrope walker traversing a canyon while high in the air, carrying a long pole for balance. The pole helps the walker balance, but it is not magic. The person makes the decisions. The feet do the walking, but the pole enhances the walker's stability. Could the tightrope walker walk the tightrope without the balance pole? Probably not. He or she would walk with arms extended, a poor substitute for the balance pole. The walk is much easier with the pole. In the same way, we seek to find balance through the questions we ask, hoping to produce an answer that brings balance to this grieving process. Balance may come through answers, information, thoughts, or beliefs. We say that our loved ones lived a full life, that they died doing what they enjoyed, or that their suffering is over. These are truths that we focus on to provide a little more balance, perhaps lengthening the balance pole. But the journey of grief continues to be a tightrope walk from one side to the other.

Asking why declares that we believe someone is behind life, overseeing every circumstance, and we want their answer for death. If there were no belief in the divine, there would never be a reason to ask why. The search for meaning in death is important but difficult to conclude. Can death have a greater purpose beyond creating sorrow? Can there be a purpose exposed that will soften the blow of death? Will an answer make grief easier to live with? Does the knowledge that our sons or daughters who died in battle were killed by "friendly fire" make a difference in the grief we feel? Circumstances and facts surrounding death are helpful. If someone committed suicide, was it intentional, an accident, or murder? Does that make things different in grief? Does this mean we should look for a purpose? If there are questions, search for answers. At some point, the answers you find will need to become the ones you live with. Some will search for a lifetime and know nothing more than when they started. Some will find the justice they seek, but everyone must do (within the law) what is in their hearts. The answers cannot bring back the dead. The search is important, but ultimately we trust in a divine justice. Part of grief is the search. What happened, how did it happened, did anyone see it happen, and did someone talk with him or her before death occurred? We search for and try to discover something good that has come from the tragedy. This can add comfort or create more questions. A purpose for death may make bereavement a little more balanced and manageable. If events point to someone or something being responsible or other unusual events, then seeking answers to every question is important.

Unit 53

Change: From *Why* and *When* Questions to *What* and *How* Questions

Often, *why* questions end up chasing other *why* questions around in a circle, and we never arrive at a conclusion. So give yourself permission to ask each *why* question and find as many answers as possible. Work at keeping each request and answer separate from other questions and answers. You will know when the collective answers need to be combined, but in the present, keep them in their own categories. At some point in this cycle of questions, there is a time to stop the pursuit of why this happened, why now, and so on and move to *what* and *how*. You will begin to ask, "What am I to do now that this has happened?" and "How will I deal with life now that this has happened?" *What* and *how* questions are assessments with which you try to consider the situation and find direction. This changes the outcome of the question from seeking to place blame to looking for a course of action. *Why* and *when* questions chiefly result in arguments, where assigning blame or fault is the objective. They elicit defensive posturing in ourselves and in others. Questions such as "Why did you do that?" and "When will you get this done?" can be changed to "What is the reason this was not done?" and "How will this be accomplished?" The first two seek to blame, while the second two seek assessments that can create a framework to work from, resolving the problem.

When problems or questions are looked at from an assessing point of view (what and how), the chances of finding the solutions rise exponentially. Hopefully, by discovering a resolution that we are content with, this choice brings some form of closure. This change in phrasing questions to *what* and *how* is a deliberate decision to look at life as presented, uncovering a course or direction. The particular intent is to answer as many questions as possible and then move the focus from "Why did this happen?" to "What am I to do now that this has happened?" Remember, we are always able to look back, to think of our loved ones, to shed our tears, and to miss what is now absent. The change comes by not blaming or attacking life—which is what *why* and *when* questions accomplish—but by assessing or choosing actions for living through *what* and *how* questions. These questions rotate the focus to today and tomorrow. Whenever we walk backward into the future, we trip over the present, and when we are constantly tripping over today, it is time to rotate the focus to what is happening around us. Life is changing again. Tomorrow is coming. Let us do our best to prepare ourselves to greet life today. What are we to do with the life before us? How are we going to accomplish this?

Unit 54

Random Acts of Violence

Why questions can dominate grief, especially if the death was the result of a random act of violence such as a drive-by shooting, indiscriminate bombing, murder, driving under the influence (DUI), car accident, domestic violence, and so on. All of these and more are senseless acts resulting in perplexing deaths. There is no apparent reason for the death other than it was a willful act of an individual or group. As a society, we try to govern actions by making laws that take away guns or keep drunk drivers off the road. There is often someone to blame but no one responsible. The "greater good" or "personal rights" of habitual offenders allow the random acts of a drunk driver or a mentally ill individual with a knife or a gun to take lives. We pass laws to govern actions but refuse beliefs that govern the heart. It is from the heart that the responsibility to care for our fellow man arises. Senseless death causes such a demanding grief as those left behind search to find a purpose for such an action—something, anything that could explain a senseless act. We struggle with emotionally charged perspectives, such as gun control, as if we could eliminate death by guns or the emotionally charged perspectives on zero tolerance for driving under the influence as if we could eliminate death by alcohol. We know that if something had been done, our loved one might still be alive. Who or what do we blame—the liquor industry, gun manufacturer, auto industry, a lack of safety, a lack of laws, inadequate oversight, carelessness, willful neglect, bad roads, a snowstorm, a rainstorm, a hurricane, gas cans, farming, pollution, gas wells, the medical profession, God, the church, bad karma, society? Where does the blame lie? There is often someone to blame, even the individual who died. "If he had only stopped smoking," we might say, or "If she had stopped drinking." There may be someone to blame but no one responsible.

Details of what took place in many circumstances are extremely important. If there are medical questions, ask the physician. If there was an accident, request to speak with the officers who were at the scene. Know what happened, what was done, what was not done, and the reasons for the actions taken. If there are blank areas of information, we tend to create our own scenarios in our minds. Imagination will fill in the blanks with incorrect information, leading grief on a ghost trail where neither the ghost nor the trail exist. Collect as much information as needed to satisfy the questions. It is important to understand as much as possible about what transpired. No matter how much we ask or seek and no matter how much knowledge we acquire, there may still be some questions that will never be answered, but seek to answer as many questions as possible.

Unit 55

Reestablish Life

*H*ow will I reestablish life and relationships? you may wonder. *What does the future hold for me?* Now, when speaking of building relationships, I am reminded of individuals who felt that life beyond loss was impossible. *There is life after death for the bereaved.* These people felt that living had become an impossible task given their individual lives of forty-plus years with one person and the "hopeless" assessments they had of themselves. Today, one person in particular states that he would "still be living on a dead-end road if it were not for the time and thoughts presented in group." The death of your loved one is not the lead story in building your life. In the initial segments of grief, death was the headline; everything revolved around death and sorrow and grieving. With time segments and the struggle of grieving, life has changed. The outlook now is not so much on what was lost but on what you had, what your loved one meant to your life, and the strength he or she gave you to go on. You are grateful for a life that was and recognize the value of what is. In present relationships, now is the perfect time to inform loved ones that they are treasured and valued in your life. It is like a two-sided coin—on one side is loss, and on the other side is life being lived. That is why grief appears to be flipping, changing, rotating, spinning, and choosing which side you will experience today. Is it from death to life or life to death? The *why* questions have changed, suggesting the expectation for something different. The change from *why* to "What am I to do now?" makes your search an expectant one.

Unit 56

Remembering

How could someone not remember the love of his or her life? The concept of forgetting somehow becoming a goal in grief is completely wrong. Perhaps the idea has its origin in the faulty logic that to stop the grief and pain, we have to stop the memories. This is *false*. If you love someone and that person dies, you will miss him or her. This is grief, and this is life. One individual who was very close to his older brother had never known life without him. They were friends throughout their childhood and teen years and as adults. Their pattern of contact as adults was daily; they spoke on the phone or met for breakfast. When the older brother died unexpectedly, it left the other devastated. "It has been three years now since his death, and I think of him every day," the surviving brother said. "What is wrong with me?" If you interacted with a loved one in your everyday life, death will not change that desire or that pattern of behavior. In grief, you will continue to think of that person every day as you had done before. Thought patterns, daily routines, and relationships do not change because the loved one is physically not available for a phone call or breakfast. Love establishes its own borders, which exceed all other boundaries of time, space, and relationship. Thinking of your loved one fifty years after his death and missing him is normal. Life has changed; it is nowhere close to what it was at the time of your loved one's death, but in your heart and mind, there is that place that holds his or her memory, love, and friendship. Do not try to evict the resident because of death, pain, or grief. The memory of one loved will be with you for a lifetime. Cherish the memories and the experiences. You cannot physically return to them, and you cannot live among them again, but they were places and times where this person was loved and he or she is missed. The feelings will intensify at nine in the morning when you met for breakfast or at eight in the evening when you made the call.

If someone is no longer physically present, your mind does not suddenly shut off your thinking of him or her. After the death, what would stop your thought pattern of wanting to speak to your brother or other loved one every day? He died, yes, but how does that stop the mind from wanting to maintain the pattern of speaking to him? You want to give and receive as you did before the death; it was important to you. You miss your loved one, the phone call, the assurance he or she gave, and the friendship shared. This is who you are and who he or she is to you. What changed? The relationship and the memories are still there, and you will forever miss your loved one because of the relationship you shared for fifty years or however long. So even though the memory patterns do not end, they do change. If you have done the same thing every day for years, your mind is set in that pattern. Your mind will initiate the routine without your even thinking about it, similar to autopilot on an airplane. You have set the course, and the plane can fly itself. That is why you may pick up the phone to call someone and then remember that he or she died. Grief is the merging of the old routine with the new reality of a loved one's separation at death, which brings grief, sorrow, and a pining for them. Does memory change because someone has died? The memories are forever there, and the circumstances as they happened cannot change. They are entered into our memories; they are written; they are photos on the pages of our minds. The change is in the way we view them.

The grieving brother I mentioned earlier expressed concern over the fact that he believes his brother is in heaven with God but he still has a concern: "Why do I have this frustration with his death if he is happy in heaven?" The frustration is not with where his brother is; the frustration is with the ongoing pain associated with the separation and the memories and with knowing that he will not see or hear from him again in this life. We miss our loved ones. At some point, the memories will create a feeling of comfort related to the life we shared, but not today. It is difficult in the midst of sorrow to inject the thought of being grateful, but in grieving try to also see the privilege of having had the friendship or relationship. In our personal sorrow, we can place the thought of gratitude for what was shared. It is difficult to conceive, but not everyone has such a special gift. In sorrow, we value what once was; this is a perspective of life that was not visible before. This is not a "stop grieving and be thankful" declaration. I am suggesting that we interject an aspect of thankfulness for the life lived. We are not thankful that our loved ones died; we are thankful that they lived and that we were part of their lives and they a part of ours. Gratitude helps in bringing balance to grief.

Will we always miss them? Yes. Trying to force yourself not to think of someone is like forcing yourself not to think of a pink rabbit. Your mind immediately thinks of a pink rabbit. Pressure to push someone from your mind is essentially pushing his or her memory to the forefront, so pressure is not the answer. We do become tired and weary of feeling sad, but trying to push something out of the mind—essentially evicting it—only generates more of what you are trying to avoid. Trying to force grief from the mind is like standing outside in a rainstorm, getting drenching wet, and trying to force yourself to think, *It is not raining, and I am not wet.* Why not recognize that it is raining, wear the appropriate rain gear, finish your outside project, and then go in out of the rain with the knowledge that it will stop and the sun will shine again? With time, the expression of grief, and the expression of thankfulness for having this relationship, comfort will return. The past can never change; what changes is the way we think of and view the past. We are open to all thoughts, especially gratitude for the life shared.

Unit 57

Belongings

Give yourself time to sort through the belongings that were once part of your and your loved one's life. Give yourself permission to hold these belongings and to remember. Carrying out the task of removing another's things is an important undertaking. What lies before you are the things that represent a life. Not only do they represent the deceased, but they are also connected to the memories and actions of when they were worn or used by the deceased. This process of sorting through a loved one's life should take place when it fits your life and your grieving experience. It may be weeks, months, or a year after your loved one's death, but "when" is not as important as "how" you sort through belongings. Take time to remember, to touch, and to smell their things, and have someone with you who will journey with you to when this special someone wore the garments or used the items. Speak often of the loved one.

Give permission to yourself to gift certain items, to help others with donations, or to sell valued things, and use the money to get a special gift for yourself or a favorite organization. This sorting will be a stopping place along the grief path. Since your loved one's death, these belongings have been handled, thought about, and placed back, but at this time, a decision is made to sort through, give, and sell things. You will know when the time is right. Purposeful recollection can be helpful—looking at a family album, wedding pictures, vacation pictures, movies, and recordings; speaking of past events with family and friends; crying, laughing, and feeling sad and happy that you were so fortunate to have had such a life. One widow spoke of how her husband's things sat on the floor exactly as he had placed them the last time he got out of bed. For months, she never moved the clothes, and then one day she decided it was time to wash them and hang them in the closet. It was not until sometime later that she and her daughters decided to go through his things. It became a day, the widow stated, that she would never forget; all the memories the three of them shared were supportive and comforting. They were remembering the man and the impact he had made on their lives and the lives of family and friends. These good things remembered are the goodness and mercy spoken of in the Twenty-Third Psalm that shall follow one's life.

Unit 58

When Do I Remove Belongings?

Regarding this question of removing a loved one's belongings—when is the right time?—the answer is, when you are ready. One misconception concerning clothing and other personal belongings is that if you get rid of the belongings, you will get rid of the pain. Belongings represent a person, and when we see or hold them, the attached memories come back. The misunderstanding of grief, sorrow, and things is that if there is to be progress, you must remove the things. This is not true. In fact, having things can be helpful in grief, as specific memories can be attached to certain objects. The things around you stimulate memories of your loved one, such as the empty chair, articles of clothing, the home you live in, or the car you drive. Each area of life contains memories, and that is not a bad thing. Holding articles of clothing, remembering when they were worn, and attaching memories and sorrow to them is a good thing.

Removing a loved one's belongings is a personal decision. May I suggest, again, that you do so when you have time to hold, remember, tell stories, and gift them to another. This particular step of "getting rid of those things" attracts numerous advisers. There is pressure from well-meaning family and friends who feel that clearing the house of the deceased's personal belongings would stop the crying and would be a sign of moving forward. But if there is no rush, why force yourself to be in one? Will getting things out of sight make that much of a difference? There is no rush or push to get things out. The clothing and other items do not create the pain. They remind us of the loss, the death of someone we love who is no longer here to wear the clothes and live in the house. Removing belongings is a task that is not rushed but is done with remembering, touching, and smelling that reminds us of our loved ones. These items remind us of their lives and their absence, but they also comfort.

There are many different ways to approach this. I know of situations in which family members have gone to the bereaved's home and removed all the belongings while the bereaved spouse was not home. When the bereaved returned and saw everything gone, he or she was devastated. It created another great loss. The emphasis is not on getting over someone's death; the emphasis is on dealing with aspects of this person's life that we now miss. Going through the clothing and personal belongings of our loved ones is a very important process. In some situations, spouses have found letters written to them by the bereaved before they died. These letters contained words of encouragement and words of love. You will know when the right time arrives. Remember, your memories are more important than things. The emotions that connect these memories are important. Being able to hold these memories in an article of clothing or in a special possession will at first bring tears and sorrow, but with time, many have found comfort in what once brought sorrow. In bereavement discussion groups, it is a pleasant surprise to the group when they hear others speak of wearing an article of clothing that belonged to the deceased, of how many would sit in the deceased's chair, or of how many could never sit in the chair or sleep on the deceased's side of the bed. They find comfort in the little things that remind them of their loved ones.

Many stories have been told over the years, stories like the one about the radio left on the nightstand that the individual who had died would always play first thing in the morning and last thing at night. When the person died, the surviving spouse could not touch or listen to the radio because it brought her so much pain. After a few months, she turned it on one day, and she did so with tears and a smile. Then she played that radio every day, and it brought her comfort. Others have spoken of shoes or articles of clothing that their loved ones wore for the last time still setting in their special places. At first, the articles of clothing were not moved, as if waiting to be worn again. With the passing of time and conversation, they felt it was all right to move them. The goal is not the moving or touching of the objects but of recognizing the emotion, the memory that is associated with these personal items. There is no rush and no push, but someday, not today, you will share these belongings with others. *I know it is what she would have wanted*, you may think. When the time is right, hold these cherished articles and feel close to the one who wore them, and then give the articles of clothing to someone in need or sell items like tools or a vehicle—but when it is right for you. Remember, once given away, the things belong to another and will not be cherished as they once were. They do not have the same meaning to the new owner as they once did for you.

In the first segments of grief, it is normal to keep things as they were, having pictures and other effects just as they were before the death. But if time passes into years and nothing has changed, nothing has been moved, and the house has become a sacred shrine revered as a holy place for the deceased to dwell, there is a need to speak with the bereaved about how this came to be. This is not a good thing. One such story is of a spouse who made a shrine to the deceased, with pictures and candles, and she went through a daily routine dedicated to the deceased. After four years had passed, she was in a relationship that had developed to the point of marriage, but there was a problem. Because of the shrine, she had the feeling that she was cheating on her deceased spouse, and that halted the relationship. She sought counsel and concluded that, in the early grief experience, the shrine and associated routine were a way to help in the recovery process. But now, acknowledging that her marriage vows—"till death do us part"—were complete, it was possible to proceed with her present life. The items of the memorial that occupied the shrine were carefully, lovingly dismantled, and a few pictures or items were left out for all to see.

There is no competition with the life that was; there is simply life as it continues to be. The past is always with us in our memories, and the present is life as it is now, a combination of what was and what is. And the future is a dream for discovering as we walk into tomorrow. Remember, when someone is part of your life, that person will always occupy that time and place. The memory of that time and place can never be erased or dismantled. Should there be another who comes into your life, that person is not a replacement; he or she is an individual who is loved for who he or she is. That person loves and lives in a time and place that is present—today. Memory can never be erased or pulled apart. The challenge and difficulty comes when time has passed, and memory tries to be today's reality.

If you happen to be an individual who had your loved one's belongings hastily discarded, please do not take that action in a negative way. People who wanted to help make life easier for you had a misconception that this is what needed to be done. Their intentions may have been right, but the action still hurt. We make decisions based on what we know and think is right at the moment. We cannot go back and change anything, but we can remember and deal with the present in a restorative way. Allow this present moment to be a healing one in which you remember to hold all relationships as special treasures in your heart.

Unit 59

Critics

Critics are fault-finders, the self-appointed individuals who sit in the armchairs of life criticizing, critiquing, and complaining, all the while trying to direct the lives of others. They have little experience and no firsthand knowledge of the subjects about which they preach, and they refuse information that would contradict their preconceived notions. Such a critic is not a person who thoughtfully offers constructive considerations or ideas on an easier way to accomplish tasks—consider these individuals the "good guys." The critic I speak of has little understanding and an opinion on everything. Some of these "expert" critics will seek out vulnerable targets, and people in grief are particularly exposed. Critics pass judgments without facts and use manipulation to reinforce their thoughts on how you need to perform. They have little use for the facts.

The exploiter comes prepared with a bucket of topics, much like a bucket of tennis balls, and serves each one over the net, waiting for you to respond to one. When you do, that thought becomes his or her opening to heat up the emotionally charged subject with miss information, leaving you to wonder, *How did I get sucked into this?* The real difficulty arises if you begin to believe the thoughts of the exploiter. A truly unscrupulous exploiter may try to become the filter through which all of your relationships are screened. No one gets to you except through him or her. Often when that happens, this person will seek to become your only relationship by introducing uncertainty in trusted friends. He or she may offer gossip and lies to build barriers "to keep you safe," but all along this person is building a prison to shut others out and you in. Your trust level for any relationship outside of the one with the exploiter is gone; no one else is to be trusted, and he or she will continue to reinforce that decision with misinformation and lies from out-of-context stories. This person will take you for everything you have, and when it is all gone, he or she will walk away, blaming you for the failure. Such a person's greatest desire is to have you follow his or her decisions, and when (not *if*) you fail, it will be your fault that you did not follow through exactly as you were instructed. For the critic and the exploiter, their lies are always better than truth, and truth is a perception that can be changed. They consider the world to revolve around themselves and their need to control another's life. If you have what they want, they will take it from you by any means at their disposal. I have seen these individuals manipulate to the point of taking entire estates and separating families to the point that they still do not talk. Give no place to a critic or an exploiter.

Unit 60

Corrupt People

There are unscrupulous people trying to locate the vulnerable. Not only do you have the death and loss to deal with, but you must also stay alert for the scam artists, watchers, and gossipers who are all looking for an easy target. Be wise with your choices, and be careful about what information you release. If someone pushes you to make a decision, chances are that it is not in your best interest. Critics, as I said earlier, will find fault, have an opinion about everything, and try to convince you to believe as they do. They have arguments for every aspect of life. If you are upset, so are they; if you are in tears, so are they. They are so convincing that you would think you have found a soul mate straight from heaven. (They are not from heaven.) They can recite all the reasons you should trust them. Remember, if people have to convince you to trust them, do not trust them. The feeling they try and engender in you is that "you would be a fool to miss this opportunity." Some professionals sit on the sideline waiting and searching for victims to come along. They promise to solve every problem if only you will agree to follow their directions. They specialize in putting together solutions for the difficulties they observe in you and in your home, creating a believable story that plays on your emotions and manipulating the truth to fit an agenda that truly benefits only them. You can see that I have a real dislike for these actors who play the role of a comforter "just coming to help." They gain your confidence by misrepresenting themselves in a very vulnerable time, but what they offer will create isolation, distrust in everyone and then, confusion, and more pain. They have stolen people's lives, turned families against one another, abused friendships, embezzled by becoming legal counsel or taking on power of attorney, and depleted estates, leaving families without a dime. In one situation, the thief posed as a contractor, and he knew that the victim's husband had died. He went to the widow, now alone, when her adult children were out of town, and told her that as he was driving by, he noticed that the bricks on her home were bad. He diagnosed the problem as "cancer of the brick" and said that unless she did something immediately, she would lose her home. She went to the bank and withdrew $15,000 for this man to save her house. He pressure washed half of the house and said she was safe. A few weeks later, he returned and alleged that, in fact, she had not acted quickly enough and said she once again needed to save her home. She went to the bank to withdraw another $15,000, but the bank teller was a friend of the family and inquired, "If you do not mind my asking, why would you need $30,000 in cash in less than a month?" When she explained the story to the teller, he called the police and they arrested the scammer. If a friend had not inquired, this widow would have handed over $30,000 to have her house pressure washed. The stories of deceitful people plundering the lives of others are endless. Be wise in choosing who you trust. If it does not feel right on the inside, seek advice from trusted friends. Know when to walk away, and always seek reliable counsel.

Deceitful people are sightless people trying to convince their victims of their own blindness. These individuals will call on the phone and bully their way into taking money or anything else they can swindle through of a phone call. Never give your bank account numbers, credit card numbers, or social security number to those who call you, and never open your computer to a stranger who claims to be calling to make a repair. Hire a bookkeeper or accountant to help with your money, even if it is only to balance the checkbook; this person can assist in validating any request. Individuals who isolate you from others do not have your interests in mind. The isolation maneuver concludes with, "You do not need the advice of others to make this decision." Books have been written about people who have been deceived and the reasons they felt they were not being swindled. They were dealing with experts, professionals who cheat unsuspecting people. Be very careful about whom you let into your life and into your home. One lady allowed a group of young girls into her home who said that their car had broken down, they were cold, and one needed to call her dad. When they left the house, they took the woman's purse and drove off. She did not notice that her purse was missing until sometime later. Not everyone is who they say they are or there for the reason they claim; check people out. Do not be foolish with your possessions. Take precautions with your accounts, and see your local bank for advice. One person who did not believe in keeping his money in a bank hid his money in the sweeper. When a door-to-door salesperson came to sell a product, the soon-to-be victim brought the sweeper into the room and pulled out thousands of dollars to pay for the purchase. After the ensuing robbery, in which only the sweeper was stolen, the victim said, "He seemed like such a good man."

Unit 61

Spectators

Another group is the spectators. They are the absentee people—acquaintances who suddenly take an interest in you or your family after a death. Spectators invite themselves into the home with an insignificant gift or simply an "overwhelming" desire to help. They have never been inside your home and suddenly take an interest in your life. They enter under the pretense of helping, but all along they watch the interactions, listen to the conversations, and ask questions for which they have no reason to know the answer. These spectators will take anything they can consume and use it as gossip with all who will listen, implying that they have inside information. Trust your instincts; do not share personal or family information with everyone. There are only a few people, one or two individuals, with whom you need to be transparent. If private information becomes public knowledge, someone is dishonoring your trust. The best answer in grief is, "I have my good days and my bad days. Thank you for your concern." This is not a harsh, slap-in-the-face reply, but if someone was not concerned with you or your family before, why is there such an interest now?

Beware of those who come bearing gifts *and* want to stay. If people bring gifts and desire entrance into the house, stop them at the door, thank them for the gift, and politely tell them that you're too busy for visitors at the moment. Supportive friends will not intrude when their presence is unwelcome. Trusted friends who come in this sad time offering gifts of food or help leave the decision of whether they are needed to you and the family. Do not share your schedule regarding work or travel with acquaintances; it is no concern to others, just close family or very close friends. Grieving is a place where love, friendship, and understanding are needed most. There are those who can help, and there are those who will take advantage. Let the wisdom you have gained in life guide you.

Unit 62

Reprioritizing

You may feel that death dominates your existence. You are somewhat active, you get to work, maybe you even took a trip, but it feels as if what your life was is now like clouds on a windy day—blown away. Life once stretched out in many directions to family, friends, social groups, work, travel, church, clubs, recreation, and other happenings. Perhaps you have not noticed, but these areas still exist. They have not gone away; they have only been demoted, viewed through a different lens. The importance of our past actions, the ones we engaged in prior to the death of our loved ones, begins to emerge from the shadow of sorrow. The activities once thought to be invaluable, that life would not be worth living without, have now changed. They are seen as activities, not essentials; that which is of a greater value is gone. The old cliché "you don't know what you've got till it's gone" is correct. Life is the greatest gift, not life's activities. Grieving and grief advance to the new normal, and grieving takes on the reprioritizing of all things valued in life. This is not a planned change, but a transformation or an alteration happens. Things we could not live without do not hold the same meaning as they once did. The things strongly debated and contended for hold little interest. In life, we are juggling many balls, keeping any number in the air and then adding another and another. If we drop some of them, they will bounce back, but some of the balls are made of glass; once dropped, they shatter, never to be the same. Death has come and shattered one of the valued "balls." The overwhelming loss causes all the balls to fall. Fortunately, the other glass "balls" of close family have not shattered, but grief forces a prioritizing so that only the glass balls are part of the daily juggle for a time. Their value has increased; they are rare and precious, and we hold them closely. The world has not changed, just the way we view it.

Remember that you are loved not because of what you can do but because of who you are. Let that person come forward. The Message reads at Matthew 11:29–30, "Walk with me and work with me—watch how I do it.

153

Learn the unforced rhythms of grace. I won't lay anything heavy or ill-fitting on you. Keep company with me and you'll learn to live freely and lightly" (emphasis added). The "Message" allots Jesus as speaking these words to those who were laboring under the law, trying to please God, and agonizing to make life right. They were failing and becoming weary and fatigued with life and religion. Jesus wants all to join with him in living a life that is full and free, life that is lived by the "unforced rhythms of grace." Grace is the divine favor of God; there is nothing we can do to make God love us more and nothing we can do to make God love us less. He simply loves. Live with "the unforced rhythms of (God's) grace."

Unit 63

Social Friends

S ocial friends are the people who are familiar with you at work or through a network of associates. These individuals will be somewhat familiar with you but have little contact with others in your family. They are aware that a loved one has died, but they have not experienced any personal loss with the death of your loved one. These people find connection to the deceased only through you and will move very quickly away from your grief. This is not a criticism, but they have not experienced this death themselves; the only loss they have is what they see in you. What has transpired in your life is separate from what has happened in the group. I bring this up because many bereaved expect their coworkers to be understanding and supportive, but they, for the most part, are not. After a few days or weeks, they will be going on as if nothing has happened, and for them, nothing has. Many coworkers are emotionally unavailable; only those who have experienced this type of significant loss will understand what you are going through, but they may not desire to relive their own personal tragedy, especially at work. As a group, only a few will connect to your grief.

One woman spoke of giving support to a close friend who had experienced a personal tragedy. Sometime later when she needed help with her own grief experience after the death of her spouse, the friend who had practically demanded her help earlier now had no time to offer support. The "friend" declared that she had finished with her problem and did not need to take on another. The grieving widow felt that she had been abandoned and that her grief was a problem for others. In times of difficulty, we begin to understand our personal perspectives on life and the attitudes, personalities, and perspectives of others. Some acquaintances will just be too busy, but do not write all friends off. Give time for the good people to rise to the occasion. Denial that death has come into a friend's life is, for some, a kind of defense, as if death will never enter their own lives. Sorrow is a demanding experience to deal with. A sorrowful experience can make others feel uncomfortable, even if they are not emotionally close to the loss.

Sorrowfulness is deeper than just feeling sad; it penetrates the core areas of life and makes the grieving feel vulnerable. They become susceptible to life, which has proven to be uncontrollable. What is controllable is the response to social friends. They will continue to seek the person you were before death arrived. In time, that person will return, more or less, so do not burn the bridges of relationships. Being distant for a time may be all that is needed. They may or may not understand, and that is okay. You cannot fix them; you cannot teach them what it is like to have a loved one die. That person they look for has changed. Is it permanent? Certainly that person is grieving, and good friends will allow for the change.

Unit 64

Tears

While in the company of others, what happens if you cry? Tears may flow, and you will know quickly if this makes others uncomfortable. They will apologize for making you cry, and they may even walk away. Speak up in a reassuring way about the importance of sharing the past with those you know best. Express how glad you are for this person's being supportive with your tears and memories. When you are in a place where tears are not acceptable especially early on in grief, this becomes difficult. You become afraid of seeing a familiar face, the mention of the loved one's name, or remembering the last time you were both at this gathering place. Be prepared, have a way home, excuse yourself so you can get composed, or, if you can, divert the tears until a later time. And when you are in a safe place, take the time to remember the evening and the setting and cry. This is not denial. You were at a social gathering, and it takes time to adjust. Unexpected things can happen. If the waiter starts to seat you at a table where you regularly sat with your loved one, speak up and request another table, if you desire. Do not allow the past to keep you from enjoying the present. Make adjustments. When you get home, write about your memories at that table. Never hide from—but perhaps delay—the memories. Later, when you arrive home, ask yourself questions about the experience, not *why* or *when* questions (they are arguments) but *what* and *how* questions (they are assessments). "What is it that brings such awkwardness to this place?" "How will I deal differently the next time?" Note that tears can be thought of by some as a sign of weakness shown only by the fragile. It's sad to say that many hide this expression of grief as if it were something to be ashamed of or as if they were flawed. Tears are the natural expression of a broken heart. It is sad when a heart weeps; few will embrace this experience with love and understanding. If you are moved to tears and the person you are with apologizes for making you cry, pause and thank him or her for allowing you to share this moment with them. Bring the person in to the place of friendship so there is no need to feel awkward. Do not apologize for tears; help others feel comfortable with their memories and yours. Ask if they remember when something involving your loved one happened in that place. Involve them.

Unit 65

Helping Others Help Me

It may sound out of place to suggest assisting others in helping you. I can imagine the alarms going off: *Here I am in the most difficult time of life, taking everything I have to make it through a day, and you are suggesting that I use my energy to help others in the hopes that they will in some way know how to help me?* Yes. As you have probably already experienced, people who were comfortable around you before the death now may seem to be very uncomfortable. The topic of death makes people feel uneasy and anxious, and grieving is way out of their comfort zone. People in general are at a loss; they cannot even begin a conversation about death, grief, sorrow, or loss. They fear the topic, making a mistake, and making things worse than they already are, so if someone is to help them overcome these fears, it can be you. One person stated, "I do not want to be around anyone who is grieving, I cannot handle that." Then I remember a widowed saying, "I feel like a leper, and no one will come near me." When you feel like a leper, you are partially correct—you are being avoided. So here we are, the bereaved, in this place called grief, having experienced the death of a loved one. We feel alone because of the absence of someone we love, and our family and friends will not help because they are afraid of the subject of death and grief. The "burst-ers" burst into your life, burst off information, and burst out the door. It was a traumatic event, after all; they could have caught the "grief sickness" if they had stayed too long. Hopefully, they took time to breathe in the middle of bursting, but they knew they had to do something to help, and that was it. It is better if you help them speak with you and be helpful to you. As the recipient of their "gifts," it is not polite to refuse but you can redirect: "That is so kind and thoughtful, but what I really need is ..." or "Would you be so kind ..." Avoidance by others has little to do with who you are as a person but with what you are experiencing.

People in general are unfamiliar, ill informed, or willfully ignorant about grief, imagining that they can govern life with a superficial awareness and keep life at a soap-opera level of realism, which abandons all unwanted experiences. Grief is an experience that people want nothing to do with, and when they are finally faced with it, they question how such emotions can exist in a modern society, especially in a modern medical society that denies death or at the very least feels that death is an option that can be postponed to a later date. For them, grieving is felt to be a choice. As a chaplain, I was explaining hospice care to an individual who was in serious decline with a terminal illness. We discussed whether life support would be an option, where he would be placed on a respirator when he could no longer breathe for himself. He responded, "Yes, I want to be on a machine. What if I choose not to die?" At some point, death in life is not an option. And grieving over a loved one's death is not an option. It is not a selection, such as buying a soda from a machine. The answer for people who believe it is lies in avoiding the issue by avoiding the bereaved. Helping these individuals help you in your grief appears to be an impossible task; the simple response is allowing them to continue on their way until life forces the issue.

The last thing caring people want is to create more pain. They have no desire to bring up a question or statement that causes the bereaved to cry or have some type of "uncomfortable" (for them) response. Most people have a shallow tolerance or little acceptance for another's display of grief. Why do you think the terms for crying in public is "breaking down" or "losing it"? Let's define *breaking down*. My heart is broken. It is not bleeding; it is weeping. What happens when something breaks down? It stops running or stops functioning. People want to fix it. When a car breaks down, it stops running and needs to be repaired. When people are in tears, they are operating and functioning normally. They have a broken heart, but they have not "broken down." Tears are a natural, normal expression of pain and sorrow, but the only public place where tears are acceptable is in a movie theater where everyone is in the dark relating to a scene in the movie with emotions they cannot express in the light. *Breaking down* is an inadequate term. The bereaved has a broken heart, and tears are normal. The bereaved does not need to be "fixed" by stopping the tears. Can you tell me what a "chick flick" is? It is a touchy-feely movie that produces "feminine" emotions—that is, tears. A "man's" movie is a tough, beat-'em-up, shoot-'em-down movie full of fast cars, fights, and excitement but not a hint of remorse or tears. Can you see how these responses to life and loss transfer? If tears make some feel uncomfortable, remember that they are the ones in the dark, crying at a movie portraying a loss they cannot connect to in real life for fear of "breaking down."

So how, then, do we help other people help us? Frequently, individuals are looking to you for clues. They often will reflect the way you speak. Do you speak of the past? Do you speak of your loved one in relation to you only or include your loved one in their life? Do you speak of the times you were all together? Do you pause, sit with them, and enter into their conversation about their life? Do you avoid topics or focus only on certain topics? Do you use the name of your loved one in a sentence? There are circumstances that may have been or may still be uncomfortable to discuss. It is permissible to say, "This area is one I have not spoken of." It is okay to set personal boundaries as to what you speak of and how you respond. Some things are personal and private, and you do not have to tell all to anyone who inquires.

Pay attention to your internal comfort indicator. If the comfort indicator is going in the wrong direction, suggesting that a conversation is heading toward blaming, anger, or accusations; turning into a grief therapy session in a public place; or becoming a decreed "you should be doing this" instruction of which you have become the target, then stop the discussion. "This is not the place to discuss such things," you might say. Direct the discussion toward a different topic or toward the other person, with questions concerning his or her family or new things in his or her life. Change the emphasis or the direction of the discussion, or simply walk away, especially if you are at a public or social gathering. If a close friend offers to visit, set up a time to meet. If the friend does not truly desire to visit, he or she will cancel or you can cancel. Remember, if during the conversation you become sad and cry, let the other person know that it is a comfort to speak of your loved one. Highlight how much your loved one appreciated the friendship they shared or how much you appreciate the friendship the two of you share. Share memories, laugh, and cry.

It is important to keep in mind that connections with others come not so much in the stories told but in the emotions connected to the stories. The memories shared contain a fitting-together feeling (puzzle), and those feelings are rooted in the relationship. It is not a competitive event as to who can tell the best or the worst story, but speak from the shared experience of a life remembered. The familiar stories speak of what the past memories mean; this is where the emotions of love and friendship intertwine with growing support for each other. Think of the story. Is it a story of appreciation? Is it a story of connection, of giving, or of loving? Is it a story that describes the character of the person remembered? These kinds of stories and memories bring friendships and family relationships to a greater level of intimacy. The tears once considered evidence of "breaking down" are now considered as healing tears flowing from shared memories that soothe the brokenness of loss.

Unit 66

Change in Focus

The focus of life will rotate in the direction of the future: you will begin seeing the present in light of the future with glimpses backward toward the past. Some have said that they never have a day that they do not think of their loved ones. That is not a bad thing. When they were living, did you have a day that you never thought of them? Why would that thought pattern change simply because they died? Death changes a multitude of things, but some things never change. The picture on the mantle will never change, but the eyes looking at the picture will. This separating of lives will never be complete—as if death were able to erase life and as if grief were to move beyond memory. We have a personal history, written with adjoining lives, and the memories of those pages cannot be reworked so that one character is written out of the pages of our lives. The record from yesterday cannot change. However, the books of our lives are not finished. We compose new pages each day, and today's pages record our lives lived today with paragraphs composed of present-life experiences, which include memories intertwined with today's events. The focus moves from the past and turns toward the present and future.

Initially in grief, living was consumed with yesterday, but as time passes and we exert the effort to deal with present life, the gradual transition takes place. When we grieve the past, we are reliving the personal history of our lives shared. When grief overextends its deep sorrow to last many years, continuing to overshadow the present and the future, it has become complex and will need to be sorted through. When this happens, death has not robbed the bereaved of life; it is grief that has become the thief, causing the loss of the past life, stealing life's present, and erasing dreams for tomorrow. Life lived is entangled with life lost, "snared in a trap." Life must be disentangled to be set free of the trap. As one person stated, "Sometimes it is the pain of grief that makes me feel connected" to the deceased, as if, in letting go of our pain, we will lose our connection to our loved ones. When pain becomes our comfort, it is not a comfort at all. This ploy needs to be understood and its grip loosened.

At some point in the process, sorrow must give way to hope. Hope is more than a wish or a desire. Hope is a confident expectation for good. Nevertheless, today's daily events of good are often camouflaged in the sorrow of loss. If you have ever been in the woods with a very experienced woodsman, you know that they can see animals that a beginner will never see. Their expertise in knowing what to look for is extraordinary. There was a time in my youth when I was hunting deer with a woodsman, walking quietly through the woods. He stopped and pointed to three deer standing ahead of us. I couldn't see even one of them. He let me walk ahead, and they burst from their cover and started running. I saw them then, but not until they moved. This man practically lived in the woods. He knew what to look for when stalking an animal. What does hope look like? I often feel that looking for hope is a lot like hunting. Everything looks the same until something jumps out in front of you. Then is the time we say, "I wish I had seen that coming." Hope is here with us in everyday life, but it blends in with all the ordinary things and is easily missed. Hope is an internal strength, a knowing that life is good and that good is coming our way. Hope is the assurance that life will be good again.

Unit 67

What to Do with Memory

We are part of every person and every event chronicled in our memory. This is the living history of your life, recorded as experienced. Grief and sorrow have encompassed the other leading person, but your character is emerging from the cocoon of sorrow as a new person. Life continues to be written in the present tense. Today's record chronicles today's events mingled with memories. New events arrive each day declaring that life is not over and announcing that new life arrives day to day, and hope is part of the day. When remembering and reading the journal of the past, we read it as it was entered, unchanged. But today and tomorrow will be written in light of living, of hope, and of an eternal future. Hope conceives the expectancy of seeing our loved ones again. This view is where our loved ones are waiting for us to arrive. The light of the future shines back upon today as one of hope and of a life that is endless. We live each day in the light of an eternal future where all will stand alive again. The future life outshines the shadow cast by yesterday's loss, which is the shadow of death. The past can never be rewritten or relived; it is memory. It will be forever as it was. The future is an empty frame in which we envision the expectation of what will be. This expectation of the future allows the memory of what was to connect us to what will be through the present life. Life is birthed in expectation; life transitioning to eternal life births a new today and a new tomorrow alive with possibilities. We live life facing toward home—heaven.

Looking back is a good thing. Memory is valuable in remembering people we treasure and how they loved us. Nevertheless, the focus moves from past life to present and future life. My mother always spoke of her brother, Bud. He was her older brother. They were very close in age and friendship, but in his twenties, Bud was killed in a coal mining explosion. Mother often spoke of Bud, his life, his death, and his faith, but most of all she spoke of how much she missed him. While Bud died in his twenties, my mother lived to be ninety-three. Even in her nineties, she never failed to speak of how

165

much she missed Bud and how she looked forward to seeing him again. Close relationships will remain close throughout our lives, no matter the amount of time or distance. Memories bring a balance to the present and the future. Do not be afraid of the former times. You lived through them. They are part of you. Now we embrace the present with memories of yesterday and dreams for tomorrow. Remembering yesterday, combined with today's experiences, will create new memories, dreams, and hopes. All are seeds planted in the soil of life that will bring a harvest; they will be realities in tomorrow's journal.

Unit 68

Blame

Placing blame comes through the review, the reliving, and the close examination of events leading to death. In this assessment, we conclude that something has gone wrong; our loved ones should never have died. *Who is to blame?* we want to know. From this vantage point, grieving the death of a loved one has a more complete picture of events and decisions. The review has a beginning, a place where perhaps some things exist, such as the first indicator of what could happen: "I told him to stop smoking," "She always drove too fast," "Why would he not listen?" or "I told her to see a doctor." With an illness comes the measures taken to find a cure, the understanding of the sickness being in remission, the return of the disease, the hospital stay, the digression, the emotional change, the fight being over, the waiting to die. Who or what is to blame? The area that haunts us is the area where the correct decision had a chance to tip the scale in the direction of health, and it was overlooked. If only at that critical point the correct decision had been made, we reason, all would be different. Blame is seeking someone responsible for influencing or making that choice. If they had chosen correctly, perhaps our loved ones would still be alive. Blame requires little information and a lot of guilt. Deep sorrow is a dreadful thing.

Self-blame causes us to think things like, *If only I knew then what I know now, I could have made or influenced the correct choice; I should have known something was wrong; If I had turned left instead of right or if I had been a few seconds earlier or a few seconds later, the accident would not have happened; What if he had visited the doctor sooner? What if the doctor had only read the report correctly, taken another test, or referred for another opinion? What if I had only said no or said yes?* This rehearsal of possible scenarios and possible solutions that might have changed the outcome is our way of searching for that moment when things could have been done to alter the present outcome. We look for that one place where life was still within our power to change.

It saddens me to hear the stories of regret, as if malice were behind the situation. The choice to wait or to proceed was arrived at with the knowledge in hand at the time. We chose what we knew at the moment to be the best choice. Few decisions are black and white. We sometimes have to choose the lesser of two evils, the 51 percent over the 49 percent.

Blame desires a faultless process, and in apparent failure and frustration, we mourn that our loved ones died and now complicate this process with blame. There may be occasions when wrong decisions were made or someone is to blame, where the action or lack of action is directly linked to the cause of death. In those cases, such failures have an adequate foundation of malpractice. This kind of negligence is not what I'm referring to when I talk about self-blame. This negligence is where courts and laws determine the correct conduct of a professional. In the area of self-blame, there are few clear-cut legal codes to define an obvious wrong. Self-blame resides where no blame is found but where personal scrutiny has manufactured blame under the intense microscope of personal grief. There is no attorney or court to determine guilt or innocence; we have only our personal guilt bias of seeking a guilty verdict. It manifests as an ongoing search to find something about which to be guilty.

Blame, the counterpart of guilt and shame, shares the same motivation behind assigning responsibility with invented or distorted information, such as blaming yourself because you were the caregiver: "I left the room for a minute, and she died. I should have been there." Blame that seeks out an offender does not need truth to affix guilt, only an assumption. It is not wrong to remember or look at what was done, was not done, or could have been done. Remembering and questioning are good things, as are speaking to the staff at the hospital or the officer at the scene of the accident. Information is needed to anchor the emotions as to what or how something took place. The problem arises when bits of information lead to false accusations or are crafted to make a whip of assumptions that are then used for repeated beatings of others or ourselves for something that never happened. Blame and shame have no future, only a destructive past with a faulty foundation.

These "whipping" circumstances need to have answers, but for the masters of guilt, very little can stop their anger-filled lashings. It will take a willingness to view life from the perspective of others to understand actions taken. Answer as many questions as possible. Nevertheless, there will come a time when we leave all of this behind. God is the final judge. He will bring a just settlement. Forgive and let it go. Forgiveness allows you to face the future without carrying the past. Forgiveness allows peace to reside where pain and guilt lived. God forgives; let Him.

There is also a time for accepting the fact that some *why* questions have no answers. If this announcement of letting go creates anxiousness, perhaps the story needs to be explained to a professional listener. Some new ears need to hear what you are saying. Blame, if someone or something is to blame or if there is no one to blame, does not change the outcome. Forgive and move on. This is a tragic story—a few boys, all related, were playing cowboy, and they decided to hang one of the boys from the top bunk. As a parent, whom will you blame for that child's death? Is there an answer to the *why* question? Is the parent to blame for not watching the child play with other relatives in the family home? Do we blame the other children? Who is responsible? How do you go on after such a needless death? The child has died. The other children live. The relationships grow distant. A "religious" person declares, "It's God's will." Some *why* questions have no answer. What action needs to be taken? Forgive and let the past go, but always remember your child. Which one of your children can you forget? None. Certainly not those living, and certainly not the one who died. Remember, your child who has died is alive in heaven, and you will see him or her again. We grieve, we remember, and we go on with hope. The living children need their parents. We give our children to God's mercy and grace, and He will care for them until we see them again.

Unit 69

Let This Cup Pass

In the garden of Gethsemane, Jesus said, "Father, if it be possible, let this cup pass from me" (Matthew 26:39 KJV). In Mark 14:34 (MSG), Jesus said, "My soul is overwhelmed with sorrow to the point of death." What was Jesus referring to in the phrase "let this cup pass from me"? What did He not want? Did Jesus not want the "cup" of His blood, His death, His suffering, or the crucifixion to happen? No, He knew that all of this must take place as foretold in Scripture. It had to happen! Jesus even stated that it was for this reason that He had come (John 12:27). The next hours would hold the greatest testimonial of a willing sacrifice in the foulest of circumstances—His betrayal, the mocking, the false accusations, scourging, nailing to the cross, and death. Is this the "cup" Jesus was asking God to let pass from Him? Was this what caused His soul to be overwhelmed? No, I do not believe this to be the answer. Could it be the "cup" of separation from the Father? This separation would take place when the sin of the world was laid upon Jesus. From the cross, Jesus cried, "My God, My God, why have you forsaken me?" (Matthew 27:46). "The whole earth became dark, the darkness lasting three hours—a total blackout" (Luke 23:44–45 MSG). This separation that Jesus accepted brought the greatest of sorrows and the greatest of accomplishments. He accepted it so that we, humankind, would never experience separation from God. We live with God in this life, and when our physical bodies cease to function, all that is life goes to be with God. We live with God now until we live again with Him—life to eternal life—never to be separated from God.

In grief, we have a dim reflection of the agony of which Jesus spoke. The agony of Jesus is beyond our comprehension. If we were able to accumulate all the sorrow of loss that has ever occurred and will ever occur and put it in one cup of sorrow, we would begin to see a portion of the "cup" that Jesus desired to let pass from Him. This is the payment waged for humanity's sin, God's purchasing forgiveness. To do this, Jesus experienced the crucifixion and the separation that sin must inflict upon humanity. Since Jesus took this upon Himself, no believer will ever experience the hopelessness of being without God, the hopelessness of separation from God. Jesus is the Lamb of God who takes away the sin of the world.

> But it was our sins that did that to him, that ripped and tore and crushed him—our sins! He took the punishment, and that made us whole. Through his bruises we get healed. We're all like sheep who've wandered off and gotten lost. We've all done our own thing, gone our own way. And God has piled all our sins, everything we've done wrong, on him, on him. (Isaiah 53:4–6 MSG)

Now, forgiveness is a gift from God, a gift given by Jesus Christ, and as we confess our sins, we accept His sacrifice and receive His forgiveness for the failures of life. Jesus drank the "cup" of separation so that we, humankind, would never be separated from Him.

If you have ever asked the question, "Does God really know what I am going through?" the answer is yes. Grief takes us to this place of struggle; of suffering in body, soul, and spirit; of being physically in turmoil, emotionally drained, and spiritually searching. Grief wrestles with our whole person, revealing a sorrow we never knew could exist. It is here that we find ourselves with Jesus in this garden of agony. Jesus captured the cross in this place of struggle. He found the strength and knew the course that lay before Him. Jesus is with you; He knows the course that lies before you. He will not leave you, and He will not forsake you (Heb. 13:5). He knows what sorrow is like. He brings comfort, assurance, and strength for each day.

Unit 70

Worst of Times

What is the worst of times in this grieving process? It is the time when we realize that our loved ones are not coming home. To hear the news that a loved one has died is inconceivable, and to be involved in the funeral preparation such as choosing a casket or vault and planning the viewing and the burial is traumatic. It would seem as though this must be the worst of times. But there is another time further down this grief path when the truths of these events bring a realization that our loved ones are not coming home.

Once we reach this lowest point in the grieving process, life will gradually turn toward the new normal. There can be no rushing to this point or a sudden burst toward a new normal. It is time and effort and talking and doing and feeling that have brought us to this point, and the same will continue to escort us toward the future. This new life will arrive, but another trial will be faced—guilt. "If I loved him, how can I go on without him?" we may ask. "If I feel better, does that mean I did not love her?" These steps are leading to a regaining of life without the trauma of death challenging each movement. No guilt detours or guilt barricades are permitted.

Another image I think of for the grieving experience is walking along a flat, plain section of ground and then, without warning, falling off a cliff. This fall is the death of our loved ones. Once we gather ourselves, we begin this winding descent, this progressively declining, difficult path. We think, *This is the wrong way. I should be going upward, and I should be getting better.* But the trail does not lead upward; it takes us on a winding downward trek. How long will it take for our emotions to catch up with the facts that our loved ones are not coming home? Going back is not an option; there is no way back—only forward. In the valley of this descent, at the bottom, is where we reach the realization that our loved ones are not coming home. "I have never felt so low," we say. From this place, the trail begins a gradual incline as it winds upward to a plateau out in the distance. On this side of the trail, we question whether we should go on, and guilt over not grieving as we did before tries to force us onto a detour. With time, effort, talking, feeling, and doing, we find our way to the place of life that is our new normal. *I still miss my loved one*, we think. *I just express it differently now.* Looking back across this great valley, we can see off in the distance where we came from and how we arrived at this new normal.

I spoke briefly of this story earlier, but for me it portrays the great impact of grief. The story tells of a mother whose daughter was sixteen, brilliant, beautiful, charming, and a leader in her school with plans for her future in place. The mother was overly protective, always making sure that her children would be shielded from anything threatening. One day, their neighbor girl was pulling out of the driveway and asked if her friend, the daughter, wanted a ride to school. The mother never allowed such things, but on this day she reluctantly agreed; she could see the school from their driveway, after all. In the few blocks between her home and the school, boys from her daughter's class were also driving to school. What happened next is not definite—maybe it was speeding, chasing, carelessness, or just an accident—but the young driver lost control, crossed over in front of an oncoming car which hit the passenger side of the car. The young daughter seated in the front passenger seat was killed in the crash. When her mom came to see me, she was well into the initial phases of grief. Later, the mother said, "I was going crazy. I could do nothing but lie in bed and cry." For this mother, it was eighteen months after the crash that she sat in my office and tearfully said, "You mean, my little girl is not coming home?" The lowest of times.

Unit 71

Wrong Place at the Wrong Time

Decisions do not always turn out the way we anticipate. For example, one man decided to take a back road to work because of all the recent accidents on the main highway. As he drove this back road, he stopped at a stop sign. While paused at the intersection, a tree fell on the vehicle and he was killed. There were no obvious causes such as wind or someone with a saw cutting trees—it was just a rotted tree that fell at the precise moment that his vehicle stopped at the stop sign. The "comforting" thought offered by others was, "It was his time." The list of such "comforting" thoughts concerning death is endless, and the next story (perhaps yours) is more astounding. But still the question arises: "How do you make sense of this?" You do not.

I know that God is not surprised by what happens, as if somehow God could be caught unaware. I believe life to have a divine plan and a divine pattern, even if I do not see it or understand it. The lesson to learn from this is to live life until it is our time to live again in heaven. There are other philosophies and ideas, but this is where I see the Scriptures speaking peace to life and hope for eternity. Living is not just avoiding death but living life each day and making a difference where you are. I will live until I live again. Living is dealing with this present moment, the memories of past moments, and dreams and plans for future moments. We never know when life will end, and the same questions may be asked by our loved ones at our deaths—Why now? Why me? Why my loved one? Why my house? Why my family? Why my job? Why a tree at an intersection? The ultimate answer to these questions is one that will be understood from eternity looking back. Until then, live the life that is in your possession.

Unit 72

Taking Up a Cause

" I will not allow my loved one's death to be just a statistic," some say. "I will use their death to make a difference." Being moved to action on behalf of a loved one's death begins with a single stirring—his or her life and death will not have been in vain. The bereaved can be challenged with taking up a cause that will impact the dysfunction of a broken society. For the bereaved, it feels as though wrong has been recognized as right and those who want change and who initiate solutions are depicted as radical. Consider the death of a loved one killed by an individual who was drunk and willfully decided to drive. Grieving families want zero tolerance for drunk drivers, but this is considered extreme by some. The problem faced in bringing zero tolerance is in the number of individuals who did not have accidents when they drove under the influence. Among lawmakers and even among juries, there is a sentiment that favors the drunk driver, not the deceased. Many know they could be the ones facing charges had they been in an accident the last time they drove under the influence. (What a tidy phrase—"under the influence," as if forces beyond one's ability to control "influenced" the decision to drive.)

In general, people relate to the drunk driver and not the victim. They have driven when their blood alcohol levels were beyond the legal limit and know they were fortunate that nothing happened. What about parents whose children were killed by a drunk driver who went the wrong way on a highway and hit a busload of children head-on? What are the parents to do? No matter the extent of the sentence given to the driver, their children are still gone while the perpetrator and his or her family live. Life is not fair. Are grieving parents supposed to go on with life as if drunks no longer travel the highways? One comment I have heard that displays a total lack of understanding of human nature is, "Well, people who drink and drive will see what has happened and will not drive after drinking anymore." A person's nature will change only when that person reaches his or her dead end—the point when he or she asks for help. The solution is to remove their privilege to drive and fine them until they're broke. Perhaps then they will change.

Turning a heart from hatred and hurt to forgiveness and love is not an easy task, especially when death has senselessly robbed a person of a loved one and the perpetrator shows no remorse. These pointless deaths can be the result of a drunk, a finger on a trigger, a choice made by a health care professional, a virus, an infection, a political decision, a defective helmet, a loose step—the list is endless. Only God can heal the wounded heart, change a life, soften a calloused heart, instill right motives, and bring love and understanding to our lives. We have to make the choice to heal our lives or live the rest of life in perpetual contempt.

The origin of groups such as Mothers Against Drunk Drivers (MADD) is the desire to turn a drunk driver fatality into a battle against driving drunk. The following is from the MADD website:

> In the United States, the number of drunk driving deaths has been cut in half since MADD was founded in 1980. (National Highway Traffic Safety Administration FARS data, 2012. See more at: http://www.madd.org/statistics/#sthash.6CfG7DHs.dpuf)
>
> In 2012, MADD served more than 61,000 victims and survivors of drunk and drugged driving crashes. (See more at: http://www.madd.org/statistics/#sthash.6CfG7DHs.dpuf)
>
> Every day in America, another 28 people die as a result of drunk driving crashes. (National Highway Traffic Safety Administration FARS data, 2013.See more at: http://www.madd.org/statistics/#sthash.6CfG7DHs.dpuf)

MADD is a living memorial. Memorials for loved ones can be more than grave markers. They are living, active tributes creating awareness of areas of our world that are toxic. Change the neighborhood one person at a time. David in Psalm 23:6 said, "Surely goodness and mercy shall follow me all the days of my life" (KJV). The lasting legacy of a loved one is the continuation of his or her "goodness and mercy." Make a difference by refusing to abandon a cause begun by the deceased or taking up a cause after a senseless act of violence, cancer, or another deadly disease. Answering the *why* questions can be an endless spiral of trying to place responsibility or guilt on uncaring individuals who reject responsibility. (Drink responsibly.)

One group of friends at a local bar knew the police were waiting to pull someone over as they left. One individual who had decided not to drink that evening would be the decoy; he would stagger to the car pretending to be "smashed." As planned, the police officer pulled him over, and his friends drove away without being stopped. It was a clever idea, but who is responsible for the accident and the death caused by one of the friends who drove away impaired?

It would appear that death has a prejudice, that it is drawn to those who are loved. As Billy Joel and others have said, "Only the good die young," as if being good is at fault. "Only those loved are taken" is a valiant attempt to pacify grief and sidestep responsibility, as if lives were stolen because they were loved or good.

Grief is real, life is not fair, and the guilty go on living. This is the foundation for perpetual contempt, an unending disdain for life. Many of you have your own stories of unjust death at the hand of a "nice" person who made a wrong choice. Some have stories of no regret, like the drunk driver drag racing another intoxicated driver who crashed and left some dead, some injured, and a bystander paralyzed. The driver, who was noncompliant with the judgment served, went back to the same bar, drank heavily, and continued to drive. A friend of the one of the victims repeatedly saw this individual's car at that same bar and reported this to the police. For some, this is the place where you and your families have sought justice for a lifetime and found none—the drunk driver who gets a few years' probation and the loved one has no freedom from the sentence of death. Each death is different, each cause and circumstance varies, and the "just cause" you have chosen is personal. It is deliberate that the preceding stories are intense, painful, and frustrating. There are valid reasons that senseless deaths are difficult to deal with.

You visit the grave and wonder why. You sit in a wheelchair, paralyzed from the neck down, and you did nothing wrong. The hurtful anger can rage inside, but the only answer is forgiveness. There is no other option. Jesus, who did no wrong, took our place so that we would never know the senseless pain of sin separating us from God. As we relinquish our pain and sorrow to Jesus, He will heal the wounds, the scars, and the brutality of death upon the soul. I will continue to ask forgiveness for my life and forgiveness for others; I will ask for forgiveness as many times as it takes to make the hurt stop. I will forgive until the pain goes away. I will never forget. Matthew 18:21–22 (MSG) says, "At that point Peter got up the nerve to ask, 'Master, how many times do I forgive a brother or sister who hurts me? Seven?' Jesus replied, 'Seven! Hardly. Try seventy times seven.'" Forgive until the pain can no longer negatively affect your decisions or influence life in a hurtful way. Will the pain ever end? With the effort and work of grief and with active forgiveness, the pain will become more manageable, lessen, and perhaps dissipate. But memories never go away. We simply choose to remember differently. Remember the good, the lovely, and the virtue—the "who" of who your loved one was. Create good memories. Let goodness and mercy follow your loved one all the days of your life.

Unit 73

A Just Cause

The just cause has its origin in our hearts, where we desire to aid in finding the cure for an illness, preventing hurtful action, or continuing the good that another has started, such as with organizations like MADD or the American Cancer Society and its Relay for Life. Other organizations combat drug abuse and domestic abuse or advocate for gun control and road safety. The just cause is an important way to honor the memory of a loved one but is not a replacement for grieving. It can become larger than life, consuming every waking moment. Even if the cause is important, take time to grieve. You work with the cause is in honor of or in memory of your loved one, or it is a special need that is close to your heart. If every family who had a member die at the hand of a drunk would join MADD, it would make a remarkable difference.

When establishing or joining a cause, the motive needs to be a healthy one. It should not be vengeful or guilt-based. With resentful intentions, the outcomes tend toward the destructive. Vengeance will turn to hatred, and hatred will bring blindness. These damaging emotions will grow to the point that innocent people will be hurt, perpetuating the vengeful cycle. Guilt becomes a monster of manipulation, making the just cause lose its meaning and purpose. Whether you are creating a cause or choosing one, make sure you choose one that will make a difference in honoring the one you love, protect the innocent, serve those who need your talents, and give a voice to those who are not heard.

One final thought for this section is this: remember the divine declaration that all will stand before God to give accounts of their lives. In the presence of a holy God, all acts will be open and judged by the one who knows our thoughts and intentions. No random act of violence will go unpunished, and no act of kindness will go unrewarded. Affirm that which is good, stay away from that which is evil, and pray that God will give you the spiritual wisdom to know the difference. People earn the right to be punished and to go to hell, and God gives the privilege of forgiveness to all and offers eternal life in heaven. Romans 6:23 (KJV) says, "For the *wages* of sin is death;" (the wages earned from sin are the paystub that gains one entrance to hell) "but the *gift* of God is eternal life through Jesus Christ our Lord" (emphasis added). God's gift of life is eternal. No one can earn heaven; it is a gift given through Jesus Christ and His sacrifice upon the cross. Forgiveness from God is a gift to all who ask. Let us open the gift of life, receive forgiveness for our own failures, and give forgiveness to others for their failures. We can only give of what we have. Appreciate the gifts of others, and share your gifts with them.

Unit 74

Decide to Go On

To go on living without a person who has died is a decision that each person makes. It is a decision made somewhere in the heart during the grieving process. It is a decision made with the reality of loss in full view, made out of love for the one who has died, and made with esteem for the relationship with the one who is now gone. This decision to move toward the future is a decision to live and not die. This is not a pronouncement that comes at ten o'clock in the morning after which we never look back. It is a deliberate decision that comes over time, with looking back and looking to the future as we deal with our present. It is a repetitive process, this looking back, looking at the present, and looking to the future. Life can feel like being stuck in a revolving door that is constantly spinning. It is like the carousel with its horses and carts rotating and playing the same song. At some point, we need to exit. We make the decision to go on, finding a way to live in the present while looking toward the future with loving memories of life as it was.

Ecclesiastes 3:2 says that there is "a time to be born, and a time to die" (KJV). The question really is, How will I live my life until I die? In grief, can our story now begin with, "Let me tell you how my loved one lived"? Death teaches us about life, specifically that life is temporary, and the "why things happen the way they do" is left to our trust in God. Life teaches us how important it is to live each day, to love each day, to allow ourselves to be loved, and to find God's grace to be sufficient for this day. Discover God in each space of life. Do not be anxious about living; seek a place that promotes God's healing Word, where you feel loved and welcomed and in relationship with Jesus Christ. Allowing God to find us is how forgiving, healing virtue flows.

IV. Section Four

Reclamation, Repossession, and Restoration

Unit 75

Upward Slide

Have you ever slid uphill? The upward slide of grief comes after our lowest moment. (See "The Worst of Times" unit.) Our lowest emotional time arrives not as a date or a day but with the emotional and mental certainty that our loved ones are not coming home. In a few moments of time, we can move from the memory of a person's passing to wondering what life will be like in the months and years ahead. The thoughts, the memories, and the experiences will bounce back and forth from past to future to present. The experience of feeling that everything is fine and going very well will seemingly collapse with a momentary thought, and everything changes. The reason I refer to this as an upward slide is because of my experience that winter weather brings slippery roads. Extreme caution is wise when driving on a slippery, descending road in the winter. The weight of the car and the inability of the tires to grip the road can spell disaster if the car loses control and begins to slide down the road out of control. For me, going up the hill is when I try to get some speed and momentum that will take me through the icy sections and get me to the top. If you begin to slide while going up the hill, you just let off the accelerator, and the car will immediately begin to slow down. If you apply the brakes, the tires may slide, but it will require a much shorter distance to stop than it would when going down the hill. Grief at any phase can cause a "slide," but the direction of grief in the later times will cause more of a struggle trying to get up to the new normal rather than descending out of control as it was in the beginning.

Some parents whose son had died told me their story. It had been about nine months after his death, and they both decided to go grocery shopping. They said they were doing fine, met a couple of people, spoke with them, and placed a few items in their shopping cart. When they reached the end of an aisle, there in front of them was a stack of blueberry pies. They looked at each other, left the cart, and made their way to the car and then home. How do you prepare for blueberry pies? You see, blueberry pie was their son's favorite. How can you prepare for this? These kinds of events will come when you reach the end of an aisle, in the spring when the grass begins to grow, with the first snowflake of winter, and with the scent of a perfume. There is no way to prepare for them; we can only deal with them when they arrive. The upward slide is the surprise at the grocery store, the empty seat at the restaurant, the pew at church, the holiday greeting that has only your name on it, or the letter addressed to the deceased. Grief is something very familiar, but at times it just appears.

It is like falling up the stairs. We think we are established in the new routine only to find ourselves tripping while going up the stairs and falling on our faces. (This is the opposite of beginning grief, when we are at the top of the stairs and feel like we are being pushed from behind and tumbling out of control.) There is a difference between now and when the grief journey began. In the past, what took weeks or even months to work through now will take days or hours. Things have changed, and yet they somehow feel the same. The emotions are there, the same as before, but the intensity levels have diminished. What was unmanageable in the past, such as trying to stand after the tumble down the stairs, now becomes manageable. "It was just a slip-up," we may reason. It becomes easier to get up in the morning, to sit with an empty chair at the table, and to be alone in the home. The deceased is not forgotten, but the intense, out-of-control feelings are not there.

Unit 76

How Long?

I think of my wife, who speaks of when her father died; she was nine. Every December, she thinks of the day he had his stroke, of visiting him in the hospital, of staying with her aunt, and of the day they came to inform her that he had died. She speaks of the funeral and the people who came to visit, and she tells how life changed afterward. That was fifty-five years ago. We never forget, nor do we want to. Every year at the anniversary of his death, she will tell the story—some years with more details, but all with sadness at remembering her dad's death. No matter how many years pass, the events surrounding a loved one's death are remembered with sadness.

Our lives with our loved ones are past; they are history, recorded in the journals of our minds. Life with our loved ones is also present in memories, pictures, and videos; and life with our loved ones is future in heaven, eternal. They, in heaven, wait for us, but not as we wait for them. The Scripture in 2 Peter 3:8 (KJV) says, "But, beloved, be not ignorant of this one thing, that one day is with the Lord as a thousand years, and a thousand years as one day." We may live a lifetime waiting to see our loved ones in heaven, but to them, our lifetime, even if it stretches to a hundred years, is but a few moments in eternity. The value of our faith is far beyond words; it is a spiritual reality of peace, hope, and anticipation. The value of our faith in the resurrection of Jesus Christ is a guarantee of life now and of life for time without end.

Unit 77

Betraying the Past

The anxiety we feel about life becoming better can be difficult to accept. It is often accompanied with feelings of guilt as if to go forward beyond a certain point in grief is to abandon our loved ones. One person spoke of feeling as if he was betraying his past relationship: "If we truly loved someone, we could never imagine being happy again or having a new life." To go on feels wrong. But living is not betraying the dead. On many occasions, individuals within couples have stated that they planned to die first, assuming that they could never go on without the other, or that they wanted to die together and walk "hand in hand into heaven." But that did not happen or you would not be reading this; you are alive. Forcing or manipulating yourself to stay in your grief, deliberately holding back the healing of your sorrow, staying behind in honor of a past love, or becoming a martyr for love lost does not help. The goal throughout this grief process is dealing with each thought and each event as it presents itself. This refusal to recover is just another obstacle to overcome. We are not trying to forget or force ourselves into the future but to learn to live with our memories, learn to live today, and learn to plan for the future, whatever it may be. These are the same goals we would expect our loved ones to have if they were here in our place, grieving over our deaths. This feeling of betrayal is a manipulative thought that deceives the living into believing life to be a mistake. Being alive is a gift, finding love is a blessing, and giving love will bless the gift of living.

You may find yourself thinking at times, *My loved one would have enjoyed this. So am I betraying my loved one?* The answer is no. How could the love of your life not come to mind when you feel happiness and joy and you feel alive again. The times of life that you associate with these feelings are those that occurred when he or she was here. It is a natural awareness that brings up people from our past as these joyful moments of life arise. It is comparable to the empty chair at the table. When these "happy moments" existed in the past, our loved ones were there; this remembering is a good thing. We cannot forget any area of life. To continue living and discovering is a good thing.

I grew up near a small mining town on the family farm. No matter how old I get or how far from that area I move, that farm is still part of who I am, and the memories are forever part of me. I do not want to, nor can I, forget that time of my life—just as you have memories of your childhood, the home you lived in, and the areas you have lived in since. All are part of who you are. How we remember is now a choice.

Think of the list of firsts that you have encountered in the past year or years—the first day alone, the first week, the first Friday evening, first Sunday, first month, first holiday, the first Fourth of July, first Memorial Day, first Thanksgiving, first Christmas, first New Year's, the first Easter, first time to cook, first time to put gas in the car, first time to shop, first walk, and so on. All these and many, many more will have their own grief experiences. Going back to familiar places for the first time is difficult. All these events have meaning. There is a significant awareness that someone is missing. This creates an emotion, a feeling that is dealt with but that can be understood only as we reach that place, that season, that holiday, or that "first." The first time you go to a favorite store or a favorite vacation spot will each have that awareness of someone missing. One individual went back alone to the vacation spot where he and his wife had gone. For him, it was a personal decision to go and be alone with his thoughts and memories. Some individuals have yet to return to their vacation spots. We do not stop living; we do not stop going; we continue to have our firsts as we move through these experiences to the second time and the third time. It is important to remember. Remember the memories and places that brought life to the relationship, knowing that what brings us a smile is also bringing us comfort. On the tenth anniversary of his loved one's death, one person said, "Going to the boardwalk and sitting on that special bench looking out over the ocean brought a smile I will never forget."

Unit 78

Focus Forward

Know that at some point in this grieving process, the focus will move from the past to the future, to that which will be. "I have learned to live with the loss," you will say. Forgetting the past cannot happen; we cannot deal with the past to the point that the pain does not influence the decisions or the direction of today. We remember and we are sad at times, but life goes on. At first, grief is like walking backward downhill while trying to stay on a path. It feels like days or weeks or months are passing by, and all we see is the death and our loss. We know perfectly well what has happened, like we're constantly watching the same video and hoping the ending will change. We become aware that the past does not change no matter how many times we relive it. What happens when we constantly focus on the past is that we trip over the present. In the beginning of grief, the past is often our only focus. It is important to look back and remember, but in time—and remember, each person is different, so that time may be three, six, nine, twelve, fourteen, eighteen, or twenty-four months—we change to focus forward. This is often accompanied by guilt, as if we are abandoning the deceased to the past. Little do we realize at this place of turning toward the future that the people we love are never left behind. They are a part of life that will never change.

With time, the glances toward the future become our focus, and the glances we make are toward the past, although we hardly notice the rotation in our focus. This transition is not about forgetting, as if the past life never existed; it is a growing awareness of the present and the future. There can be many months of everyday remembering of certain aspects of the deceased, but what has changed is our emotional response; it is not as it once was. We have not left our loved ones, as if they are discarded or abandoned. We give consent for their memories to accompany us into the future. The memories will be attending us even if we do not consent, but giving consent asserts that we want these memories with us, that we are not fighting to push them aside or denying their existence, and we are not forcing them to attend our daily living by attempting to re-create what once was. We are engaged in living life; it will never be the same, and that is okay. Forcing the issue with thoughts like *I must remember* or *I must forget* does not work. You did not love the person because you told yourself, *I must love*. Living is the combination of everything you are from birth to this moment. The collection of all of these natural and learned qualities will be with you today and lead you into tomorrow. We allow our faith in God and His Word to hold our memories and our loved ones. We allow that same Word to bring peace to the present, letting God's all-sufficient presence walk with us through today and into the future. Every step we take is taken with the knowledge that we—and our loved ones—are safe in the arms of our heavenly Father. In this safe place I live.

Unit 79

Stuck

Another question often asked is, "Do people become stuck in their grief?" The answer is yes. "Are there people who experience abnormal grief?" Yes. If you feel that you are abnormal in your grief responses, please speak with a doctor, therapist, or counselor. If you have suicidal thoughts, seek help immediately. Grieving is a very difficult process but not an impossible one. The lowest point of the grieving process—the realization that our loved ones are not coming home—often arrives months after the death and sometimes even later.

There also can be a changing of thought from *why* questions to "What am I going to do now that this has happened?" "Who am I now that I am no longer the wife or husband or mother of my loved one?" It is never wrong to ask these questions or plan for your future. You are stuck when years of grieving have passed and you are still questioning whether life will ever become normal. One question to assess whether you are stuck is this: Do you speak in the present tense concerning your loved one, as if the conversation took place yesterday, even though he or she died years ago? An individual from a neighboring community came to a bereavement group, and she talked about her grief over the death of her husband. She explained the account of his death and funeral as if it had happened the day before, so the group was surprised to hear her say it had been fifteen years since he had died. The words she left the group with declared that grief never ends, nothing will help, everyone is lying, and it does not get any better. She and I spoke after the meeting and addressed her need to seek help. She was trapped in an area of grief that had not been reconciled, and she needed assistance that a group setting could not offer. Seeking help is a good thing. Grief is difficult enough without nursing a fracture for fifteen years.

Unit 80

Personality Traits

Another thought to consider is that personalities have a substantial impact on the grieving process. Some personalities are more reserved; they naturally hold things back. It has never been their nature to speak out or reveal themselves. However, the goals are still the same. Find ways to express your grief. The objective is learning how to be open and let down the guard of predetermined qualities that may hold you captive. Express what is on the inside. Some like painting, poetry, fishing, carving, walking, and hobbies or activities that allow feelings to be transferred. Find ways that are comfortably expressive to you. The key is allowing this openness to emerge in a safe environment. The stuffing of what needs to be expressed is like stuffing firecrackers in a hole. How long until there is enough explosive material to blow up a life?

The other extreme is the personality that talks continually. These people control conversations by talking nonstop. They can talk for an hour and say nothing about what they experience in grief, hiding behind the overwhelming barrage of words. The need here is to slow down the conversation and pay attention to what you are saying and how these words describe your feelings.

Unit 81

Then and Now

Loss can be a good thing. It depends on the personal value of the loss and the experience. If a person lost fifty pounds through diet and exercise, that would be a good thing. However, if that fifty pounds were lost due to an illness, it would be a bad thing. Everyone experiences different types of losses and changes.

When we stop to think back on all of the accomplishments, undertakings, failures, and successes that have transpired in our lives, we often develop a pattern or an outline of how we dealt with past negative experiences. Think back to some specific circumstance, such as when you first went to school. What was the experience like? What about when you, as a parent, saw your child go to school for the first time? Children experience loss when they leave home for the first time to go to school, and the parents experience loss when they see their children leave for the first time. These are very real losses and changes. There are also the experiences of moving to a new community, changing jobs, and retiring. There is the loss of a dream, the something you expected to achieve in life that now is gone. The experiences of not getting into the college you wanted, being overlooked for a promotion, going through a divorce, having a stroke or a heart attack, aging—all of these and more are losses. Some of them are unwanted, some are anticipated, but all bring change. Each one of these experiences has a personal grief expression attached to it. "Then" is loss or sorrow of the past. The present loss will one day be a sorrow of our past; it will no longer be the "now."

My daughter at the age of six was traumatized when I traded in our car. We had moved twice in a short time, she was starting a new school, and the car was perhaps the last thing left from her previous life. When I walked to the car to take it to the dealer and trade it in, there she was, lying on the hood and begging me not to take it. To this day, she keeps her cars until they will hardly run. The amount of change that goes on in a lifetime is staggering. Yet somehow, we survive. Sometimes unknowingly, we develop our own personal grieving patterns and grieving process. Some deal with change very easily, as if to say, *What were you expecting? Things can't last forever.* Others deal with change by kicking and screaming and clawing and scratching, as if to say, *What were you expecting? I wanted it to last.* It is a personal expression, a personal "thing," and one is as correct as the other.

Unit 82

Guilt and Guilt Feelings

As defined by Merriam-Webster, *guilt* is "responsibility for a crime or for doing something bad or wrong: a bad feeling caused by knowing or thinking that you have done something bad or wrong." The word's medical definition is "feelings of culpability especially for imagined offenses or from a sense of inadequacy." Feeling guilt in the grieving process is common. We feel that if something could have, should have, or would have been done, our loved ones would not have died. Self-accusations such as "If I had only known" and "I should have known" have an element of truth to them established by the *if*, but the whole truth is, how could you have known? Women often have this guilt based on the *if* impression, or the assumption that they have this "sixth sense" of knowing things before they happen. Notice that I said *impression*. Let's look at a quote mentioned earlier—"Error always rides the back of truth"—in combination with the definition of *guilt*—"feelings of culpability especially for imagined offenses or from a sense of inadequacy." Our imaginations use an element of truth as a footing for constructing guilt; it is often created to punish ourselves for a perceived failure. Many who punish themselves with guilt are the ones who bore a major responsibility as caregivers or overseers in the care of the deceased. The faulty logic, which tries to be a foundation for guilt, comes from the idea that something further could have, should have, and would have been accomplished if only they had done something differently.

There are endless scenarios for guilt, but the truth is that decisions were made, often with the input of the deceased and a medical professional, and always with the knowledge at hand. When we look back, we have the advantage of seeing the outcomes and understanding that, perhaps, if something were inserted at a certain spot, the outcome could have been different. If you want to look back, then start with the intention and the motive for the decision, the care, and the perspective embraced at the time of the decision. It is here that we find the true intention, and it is here where personal care originates. It is to this origin that guilt is taken and dismissed.

There is no crystal ball we can use to see into the future. Guilt uses a mirror, reflecting a change that somehow may have made a difference. This reflection is more manipulative, intimidating, and demoralizing than factual. This is why truth is used to dismiss guilt feelings. Beating yourself with these self-made whips of guilt does nothing to change the past, heal the present, or allow planning for the future. These feelings of guilt can be devastating; they can become captivating, secure prisons that prevent progression through the healing process. If this imprisonment has happened to you, talk to someone who can help you look at the past from the beginning forward, not from the present backward. We know that the decisions made were made with the information at hand. Had the choice been made for another treatment, would the outcome have been any different? "We should have stopped the aggressive treatment sooner," you might say. "I had no idea it would end this way." However, someone in another situation might be saying, "We should have had the aggressive treatment. He could have lived longer." No matter what the choice, guilt will turn it against you. More than just one opinion was involved in the decisions. The materials used to construct guilt are in the rewritten script of past events and their reruns as you reviewed what happened from a specific angle that highlights particulars and clearly show you as guilty of some action. Stop the reruns. The outcome never changes. Like a familiar movie, no matter how many times you see it, the ending never changes. With guilt, allow a nonjudgmental listener to stop the film, view the complete picture, and add comments to the scene. Most often, important scenes that contribute to the complete picture were omitted in guilt-filled reruns.

There is a difference between guilt and guilt feelings. We have looked at guilt feelings, but what about being accountable for your actions? If you have decided that you are guilty of a wrongdoing, the first question is, how did you come to this conclusion? Usually the one who is overwhelmed with guilt has become the judge, jury, and executioner—the self-appointed judge carrying out the punishment. *If I had not done something wrong,* the person reasons, *I would not be experiencing this level of pain.*" This is faulty logic. When you love someone and dream of a life together and then this life is shattered, grief will follow. The present outcome of death came because the illness could not be reversed or an accident occurred. The person's body could no longer support life. Faulty logic dictates that, if the outcome brought this pain, a wrong decision must have preceded the event. And the degree of guilt corresponds to the degree of grief; therefore, the bereaved is guilty by association. Again, this is faulty logic. Guilt now has a perfect setting to fester and spread—faulty logic and death. Guilt permits the retelling of the story but only as edited.

When individuals retell their guilty stories to me, I often think, *The story does not align with the character of the person telling it.* I would listen, but what I heard was not what I saw in the person; they did not fit together. I just knew the retelling of events did not match what actually happened. Remember that error always rides the back of truth. Guilt will look for some measure of truth on which to ride. Separate the story from the verdict. Retell the events as they happened, not as edited. Tell the story as it happened; look for an event or a decision that places sole responsibility on the guilty party, but then check and remember the reason for making that decision. Remembering the thoughts discussed, the information presented, and the loved one's involvement in the chosen direction help to alleviate guilt. Often, we find that it was not until sometime later that we added guilt to the story and felt that someone needed to be blamed. How else could this tragic outcome have happened? Guilt is a merciless persuader; no truth is needed.

Unit 83

Dealing with Guilt: Forgiveness

The only way to deal with guilt and its effects is to forgive. Forgiving is not declaring someone innocent. To the contrary, the person may be guilty of the crime, but forgiveness is about you, the injured party, continuing with life. Working through the process of what and how something happened is important, but it will not remove the feelings you have about who is at fault. Whether the fault lies with someone else or ourselves—if we are completely guilty, partially guilty, or completely innocent—the goal is to forgive ourselves and forgive others, letting go of all or any portion of guilt where it has found a foothold. Forgiveness is the decision to "stop picking at the wound" and allow it to heal.

I am not a fisherman, but on occasion, when my family would vacation in Ocean City, Maryland, we would rent a boat for a few hours and go fishing. Once, I caught a young skate, a fish in the same family as a stingray. When I brought the fish into the boat, I didn't want to harm it but was straining to remove the hook quickly and get the fish back into the water. The problem was that the fish had swallowed the hook, and it was lodged deep in its belly. We had long pliers to insert and remove suck hooks, but I could not get the hook out. I struggled for a while, finally retrieved the hook, and then placed the fish back in the water. My concern was twofold—had the fish been out of the water for too long, and had I killed it in trying to remove the hook? When I told this story to an experienced fisherman, he said, "You should have just cut the line," leaving the hook in the fish. He explained that the fish's stomach acid and the salt water would have eventually dissolved the hook. That fishing incident has proven to be a great way to illustrate forgiveness. It is cutting the line to the past, and the hook is the hurt created by the life experience. With forgiveness and the cutting of the line, we cannot be reeled back to that place and time. We remember it and the hook is still dissolving, but we are not attached to the rod and reel to be pulled back at someone's whim. We hurt and we remember, but we are going in another direction, away from there. Forgiveness helps in letting go of the past, healing the wound, and keeping us free to go in the direction we choose.

When it comes to God's forgiveness, it is complete. He desires only the best for our lives. God has no evil or vengeful thoughts. Every act of God is motivated by reclamation, bringing us back to a right place or right relationship. God has provided the means of forgiveness through Jesus Christ. The love God has for us is the motive behind His actions. He is "not willing that any should perish, but that all should come to repentance" (2 Peter 3:9 KJV). Repentance is allowing all the failures of our past to be removed from our lives. "For all have sinned, and come short of the glory of God" (Romans 3:23 KJV). All have failed; all have sinned in thought, word, or deed and require one greater than ourselves to remove these wrongdoings. God has made provision for forgiveness through the sacrifice of Jesus Christ on the cross. His resurrection confirms that His words are true. Jesus is the one He claimed to be. God has provided everything needed for humankind to be in a right relationship with Him. The response now lies with us. To request forgiveness from God is to acknowledge His action in providing forgiveness and our act of recognizing the need for forgiveness. This is about divine provision for the need of forgiveness and restoration. God forgives; let Him. This forgiveness is the foundation from which we can forgive.

Why forgive? If we continue to carry the wrongs of life, we will bear a heavy emotional and spiritual weight. This hinders us from becoming what God intends us to be. In forgiveness, we are casting off the weight of our own failures and the failures of others that impede our emotional, spiritual, and physical development. No longer will the past hinder our present or future. These experiences will not keep us prisoner. We learned forgiveness from God and receive forgive for ourselves. We are free from the entanglement of yesterday's failures. God can and does set us free.

Another illustration for guilt and guilt feelings is a room full of balloons, each with a long string attached, all bouncing around on the ceiling. Each one of these balloons represents a feeling of guilt. We reach up, take hold of a string hanging from a balloon representing a specific guilt feeling, and pull it down. We look at this balloon of guilt and attach it to a wrongdoing. This wrong is a real act, something said, done, or left unsaid or undone; it is a very specific act often used in punishing oneself for what it represents. This wrong act is tied to the guilt balloon. With the balloon and the act attached to the string, we take the balloon outside and, with sincerity and love, we request forgiveness from God and from our loved ones and for ourselves as we let the balloon ascend into the heavens.

Forgiveness is not an option. Forgiveness allows grace and mercy to touch our lives and, in turn, allows us to touch the lives of others. Unforgiveness ties us to the past. Guilt will keep us prisoners of past mistakes and perceived failures. Being tied to a specific place in the past is a ball-and-chain approach. This old movie replays and always has the same ending; nothing changes. The villain of unforgiveness has tied you to the railroad track of past failure. All you need now is for the train to come, blowing its whistle. The dastardly villain is laughing, and there is no one to rescue you. You have seen this movie, right? Now the good guy is you. Armed with overpowering strength, the truth of forgiveness, you break free from the cords of guilt, releasing yourself from guilt's bondage.

If the ones we love were present, what would their advice be? "Let it go and move on." The Scriptures declare that God's forgiveness is so complete that the forgiven past will never be remembered. The key word is *remembered*. We can do something that God refuses to do. He refuses to remember our forgiven failures. Forgive and let it go. Life is about loving, forgiving, restoring, and living. It is not about imprisonment by guilt. It is not about punishment for mistakes. Life is not about guilt, which is often distorted and unfounded. Discover the truth. If you have done wrong, forgive and let it go. If others have done wrong, forgive and let it go. Forgiveness replaces the feelings of guilt, anger, and malice as the balloon ascends to the sky. It is important that guilt and wrongdoing are connected, tied together, because both are lifted from our lives, never to be remembered against us again.

Unit 84

Selling and Moving

I f we were able to move to a location where death and grief could not follow, then selling, moving, and getting rid of all of our belongings would be an attractive option. I'm sorry to break the news, but this approach does not work. When someone you love dies, it creates a void, and no matter where you go, the emptiness goes with you. There was a couple who had lived in their home most of their married life, some forty years. His carpentry work was a hobby, but he was an excellent woodworker and his woodshop located in the basement of their home was exceptional. It had every conceivable woodworking tool. He made everything in their home: the kitchen table and chairs, kitchen counters, cabinets, flooring, shelves, dining room table, hutch for the dishes, couch, TV stand, bedroom furniture, doors, picture frames—you get the picture. Within a few weeks of his death, his wife decided that living there was too painful because there were too many memories. She hastily decided to sell the home and move to a nearby community. The first people in the door bought the home.

At first, it appeared to be good decision, but two months later, she moved again. She moved repeatedly for nearly two years and finally settled near a family member when her health began to fail. She said that no place she went felt like home. What we do not realize is that selling and moving creates another loss that can compound the grief we are already experiencing. Every so often, there is no other choice, and moving is unavoidable. But for this individual, each place she moved was a beautiful home, but something was always missing. The pain of grief cannot be sold, given away, or moved away from. The things or belongings that bring us pain, especially at first, will one day bring comfort. The house that is so filled with memories is initially filled with sorrow after a death, but this place is also *your* home. If moving is avoidable, give yourself some time. Take time for the memories. With moving, we lose the familiar, such as our neighbors, the store, our church or clubs, and the community. If moving is the only option, then there is no choice. But if you decide to relocate in hopes that sorrow will not make the move, you will discover that sorrow came along. It is said that bereaved individuals should not make any major decisions for at least one year. This of course is the ideal, allowing a year to move through many of the firsts, but it is a guideline, not a rule. Sometimes we have no choice.

When my dad died, my mother immediately decided that she was selling the house and moving to a high-rise. Of course, being the expert that I am, I informed Mother of the one-year plan, but my mother said she was moving! Within a month, the house sold, and she moved to the high-rise. For my mother, it was the most important decision and perhaps the best decision she could have made. The move brought her new friends, a new community, and a security that she desired. She lived in that high-rise for more than twenty-five years, and she loved it. She would cook for some who were not able to cook for themselves, she walked through the neighborhood with her friends, but most of all she just loved being with people. She also loved the sisters who were the overseers. She felt at home. I found out later that Mom had discussed this move with my dad. She had informed him long before he became ill that if something happened to him, she would not keep the house but move. This move was predetermined; it had been settled long before my dad's death. There are guidelines and information to aid in the grieving process, but each has to find what fits for them. When you purchase clothing, you do not buy the whole rack. You come with an idea of what you are looking for, where you will wear this article of clothing, what size you need, the color you want, and the price you will pay, and then you choose. In grief, one size does not fit all. Different thoughts will fit at varied times. In grief, you will make a number of choices that are particular to you. You have your own relationship with your loved one, and grieving that relationship is dealt with in your specific way.

Unit 85

Faith and Denial: Two Differing Forces

There is a difference between faith and denial; nevertheless, both involve belief. Denial is the belief that a problem or condition does not exist, while faith sees the problem for what it is and looks for possible solutions. Faith is not a stance of "Don't worry and it will be okay," as if some unseen force can make everything all right. Faith in the context of believing God is specific and based on knowing the character of God, knowing His Word, and trusting that He will work in or through our lives. Faith is looking to God through His Word and believing that His Word will provide direction for life. Faith is an understanding of God's Word applied to life. It is not riddled with guilt or manipulative behavior. God is love, a love that has sacrificed for our well-being; He is abundant in grace and mercy and more willing to give and be part of our lives than we are willing to receive. I have a very real problem, and I have a very real God.

A mistaken concept is that people of faith cannot see the problem or refuse to face reality. Jesus in the Scriptures speaks with individuals and asks some very pointed questions. To the blind man, He asked about what his need was. To the lame man, he asked what it is he wanted. To others with illnesses, Jesus would make similar requests when the answers appeared to be very obvious: they wanted to walk, to see, or to otherwise be healed. Jesus's requests of the people were specific in recognizing exactly what they desired from Him. As a bystander looking at the text, it would seem obvious what was needed, especially from Jesus. The design to have each person be specific about his or her need was paramount. If Jesus went around telling people what they needed and then performing acts of restoration, there would be no trust involved; he would be just some guy passing out candy to needy children. "Wow, isn't he nice," the onlookers would say. When Jesus interacted with those who had needs, it was the extension of faith that drew attention to His message. Faith cannot live in an atmosphere of denial. Faith is expressing a specific need and directing a specific request to God. The opposite is denial, where we no longer recognize a need or a fault, believing that acknowledgement would only weaken denial. The obvious is that I have a very real need, and I have a very real God. Denial in grief tries to bypass the pain of separation and make us project ourselves to a period prior to the loss or beyond grief, as if the death never happened. When denial extends the months into years, it blocks off areas of life as if they did not happen. This is not faith; it is denial.

Faith knows there is a need, and faith believes in a transition from where we are to where we need to be. With love and support, God and I will walk this path. I have a very real problem, and I have a very real God. I have a very real loss and a very real grief. Faith is not manipulative; faith looks for resolution. Denial creates tension, stress, and anxiety and often bases itself in fear, forcing us to retreat into a make-believe world. Faith trusts the truth of God's character as He leads us in a very real world. God is a God of love and restoration; He will accompany us through this grief. There is more to God than a glorified grandfather giving out candy.

I am reminded of the story of a class of blind students going to the zoo. Their project was to visit an elephant and report to the class what they thought an elephant was like. After visiting with the elephant, the teacher requested the students to describe their experience. One child stated that the elephant was like a tree—round, rough to the touch, and extending upward to the sky. Another stated that it was like a large bird, with wings flapping. Another said it was like a snake that curled around his arm, while still another stated that it was like a big, round barrel hanging in space. Each child had his or her perception of the elephant, and all were correct. All of us have a limited perspective of grief and a limited perspective of God, which limits our belief and restricts our understanding. Were the children wrong? No. Is our Biblical understanding of God wrong?

A great fault of Christianity is the limiting of God to certain qualities that fit our personal experience. I believe "Christian" faiths have a correct but incomplete summation of God. When we think of heaven, of dying, or of eternal life, we believe heaven to be real, but when we have to face death, we see it as robbing us of life. We believe that, somehow, death has crept in from the darkness to steal life and no one knew it was coming. Even when we are expecting death after a long-term illness with continual decline, we are still in shock when the loved one dies. (You know this is normal.) But the

Christian belief of death is the beginning of life beyond the grave; the ones we call dead are still living. Death is the door that life goes through to enter eternity. We grieve with hope in our hearts. Think of it this way—how much of our present understanding of God and of heaven has been influenced or changed since the death of our loved ones? There has been suffering, catastrophes, earthquakes, typhoons, flooding, a busload of children from a church losing its brakes and plummeting over a cliff—what changes in belief have come into our lives since death came to our homes?

Denial isolates life from the genuineness of events renouncing the complete image to believe a partial truth about the obvious. Like the blind student who held the leg or the one who had the trunk wrapped around his arm, denial establishes its own prison that restricts truth only to what is known or imagined, refusing to believe the reports from other students that the elephant is more than what they experienced. Denial refuses to complete the picture. Faith will allow us to recognize the revelation that comes through the Scriptures. This is not a blind viewpoint but one that recognizes the completeness of God's character and His interaction with our lives. We offer specific prayers asking God to make the truths of His Word real to our lives. It now is between us and God, not the words on some page in a book but the Word breathed by God into our hearts. He is the breath of life. We have in the Bible the most complete picture of God that we are capable of understanding. There is more to God than any person or religion can contain. There is more to our relationship with God than can be typed on a page. There is the person of God the Father, God the Son, and God the Holy Spirit present in and through the Scriptures that touches the understanding of the human heart. This is a relationship that a child can accept yet is so complex that the greatest minds cannot unravel it. God presents Himself to us in Jesus Christ through His love, His grace, and His mercy, which sustain life. These insights and understandings offer answers to the perplexing questions of life and death. God is forever faithful to His character, changeless, and perfectly presented in the Bible. The life of God is present in His Word born into the lives we now live, revealing God and revealing Hope.

Unit 86

Secure Life

The apostle Paul, when writing to the church at Rome, made a statement concerning life and death. "For whether we live, we live unto the Lord; and whether we die, we die unto the Lord: whether we live therefore, or die, we are the Lord's" (Romans 14:8 KJV). This is an anchor statement for living: whether we live or die, we belong to God. Paul was addressing something that was of great concern for those of the early church. They were experiencing and would experience great suffering for their faith in Jesus Christ. The Roman Christians wanted to know if going through this suffering meant that they were displeasing to God. The assurance that Paul gave to the early church also comes to us—in Christ, all of life and the life to come is safe. We belong to God. *The Message* states it this way: "It's God we are answerable to—all the way from life to death and everything in between—not each other. That's why Jesus lived and died and then lived again: so that he could be our Master across the entire range of life and death, and free us from the petty tyrannies of each other" (Romans 14:8–9). The phrase "We are the Lord's" speaks of security and ownership. "Jesus lived and died and then lived again: so that he could be our Master across the entire range of life and death" means that no matter what happens to us or around us, we are safe with our "Master." Death cannot destroy life. Life is a gift from God. We live with the events of life from the position of "I am the Lord's." At some point in life, we will all transition to eternal life in heaven. Remember, we live until we live again. The confidence of our life in Christ comes from Christ to us through the Scriptures, made real by the Holy Spirit. In the difficult times of life, know the promise of His divine presence. We live our everyday lives as one with God until our physical bodies can no longer sustain life. Then all that is life in us will go to be with God.

In 2 Corinthians 5:8 (KJV), the apostle Paul said, "We are confident, I say, and willing rather to be absent from the body, and to be present with the Lord." Paul's revelation in this verse is that, at death, we go to be with the

Lord. We live on, knowing that those who have died in Christ are safe in heaven with Christ and that we are safe with Christ here in life. Our loved ones are not alone in death. Our loved ones' bodies are in the ground, but every aspect of their alive, breathing selves are with God. God, who is the creator and sustainer of life, is not defeated with physical death. I write of these truths to give strength in the struggle of life and death, of grief and faith. God helps us to see beyond the horizon of a cemetery plot. There is truth from an eternal perspective that causes faith to rise and to see through to eternity. There is more to life than this fragmented world we live in. There is life eternal through Jesus Christ given to each of those who place their trust in His forgiveness. This truth gives hope and sight beyond the grave. An eternal view brings a different light to our understanding that connects life to eternal life. The refrain is once again stated: my loved one is in heaven, and I am here on earth. I grieve their absence from my life. My grief cannot diminish faith. My grief cannot diminish the hope of seeing my loved one again in heaven. I choose to live on in faith, knowing that all life relationships are treasured.

The focus of our treasured relationships is to inform others that they are loved. If you do not tell them, how will they know? Imagine if every time you spoke with people, you added a coin to their coin collections. After a period of time, they would have quite an assortment of coins. The sad thing is that after a long period of giving and investing, the gifts are taken for granted, and they become familiar and ordinary. Do not let the ordinary stop you. It is the little extra of your touch placed with the ordinary that makes the gift extraordinary. The importance for the giver is recognizing the value of giving and declaring the value you place on the recipients, wanting them to know just how special they are in your eyes. The key for giving is in discerning your own value. This gifting of love becomes a grand treasure because it will always remind them of you. How do you know your gift is a treasure? Think of what was familiar and valued in the past relationship that has now become a treasured memory. Now there becomes a deliberate action on your part to give to others of what you miss most of a relationship departed.

Trying to explain grief is difficult, especially to those who have little or no concept of it. The time invested in explanations will accomplish little. What you are achieving or accomplishing is not through the details of what is gone but through loving, giving, and bestowing gifts of time, listening, befriending, and appreciating everyone from the viewpoint of having learned from your loss. Giving to a young person who views life as invincible will add stability when this unshakable stance collides with loss, shattering his or her denial. Then, what you have invested will survive the shattering, and these invested gifts will be treasured.

This is not about people being sorry for how they treated you or the "someday you will miss me when I am gone" speech. If we feel the need to manipulate the present with such statements, we are likely investing in the wrong people or are going about it in the wrong way. If we need to tell people how important we are and that they will miss us when we are gone, it is time to get a life! It is time to move on and to live a little with those you appreciate and those who value your friendship. Give of what you have, even if it is just a cup of cold water to the thirsty (Mark 9:41 KJV). Those who take the cup and throw it on the ground were not thirsty and have little need of your gift. To some, our treasure may be just some old coin, but to the collector it is priceless. Treasure is for those who understand its value. Matthew 7:6 (KJV) says, "Give not that which is holy unto the dogs, neither cast ye your pearls before swine, lest they trample them under their feet, and turn again and rend you." The image of giving pearls to pigs conveys that some will never see or understand the value of what is given to them. So do not throw the treasure you possess to those who will simply trample it into the mud and turn on the giver. The pearl of truth and value given is for those who can appreciate the gift. Give the gift of love from your heart to theirs. The gift of God's love is a priceless treasure.

V. Section Five

Rediscovering Yourself

Unit 87

New Normal

Losing someone with whom you've spent much of your life is like planting trees whose shade you may never sit in, whose fruit you may never eat, and whose reseeding life will exceed your years. Do we need to be reminded of how valuable our past was and continues to be? Loss has forced the reevaluation of a joint venture that has become an individual living a life that two had undertaken. Life continues. Now, with the assurance to deal with the present and seeing the potential of others, we are moved to invest in their lives and feel inspired to share ourselves, perceiving that what we have to offer is not like what others have. We remember that the love we miss was not like anything else, and now the love we share is not like anything else. It is taking the chance to come away from this vulnerable, grieving self to share what we have learned from life and from walking this path. It is not that important if someone does not like what we offer. We will move on and give life to the living.

There are basically two types of individuals in the world—givers and takers. One awakes every morning, picks up an empty bag, and goes out to fill it. The other awakes, picks up their full sack, and goes out to return home with it empty. The world has both. Think of what could be accomplished if every time you spoke with someone, you brought good to their life, planted seed, declared appreciation, and pointed out the gifting they possess. It is finding the good, seeing the potential, encouraging, uplifting, helping them see the possibility that lies within and around them, and planting seed that makes a difference. Find something good in everyone you meet. Make it a game to count how many good things you can see in the person in front of you, and then compliment him or her. Every compliment left unsaid is a wasted thought. People need to know the value you see in them and what they mean to you.

Unit 88

Deposit

Another way to recognize this concept is that you are drawing attention to something the other already possesses. Complimenting does not deplete your emotional energy; in fact, it adds to whom you are and to whom they are. The calculated accumulative value of each interaction and each compliment given in a lifetime can never be determined. What others receive from you, they take into themselves and also pass it on. Only eternity will define the multiplied value of your actions and your investments. Make a difference now; make deposits. If we stop and consider how people have invested in us, remembering those who took time to pay attention to us and who were interested in our stories, we will see what an impact they had on our lives. At this place in life, give of who you are. Even small, random acts of kindness will add purpose and convey value—not necessarily monetary gifts but gifts from your life to theirs. Can you imagine if you were standing at the bank and someone came up to you and said she wanted to place money in your account? She would like to add this gift to your deposit slip. Now consider giving a gift that is exactly what someone needs to create a balance in his or her life account. How many people are emotionally overdrawn? In grief, you become aware of those overdrafts and how valuable the small deposits of kindness turned out to be. These actions accumulate over time. A little kindness can change the focus, even if it is only for a moment, and that moment may halt a decision that would have taken life down a different path. "Someone believed enough in me to make a deposit into my life," the recipient may say. These actions will help move the attention away from you, your pain, and your loss to help build others up. Look for the little things to compliment. Remember, a compliment left unspoken is a wasted thought.

Unit 89

By Chance

It may sound strange, but my favorite place to write is at a local restaurant. I go there and have my toast, oatmeal, and coffee. The servers know me by name; one young woman who waits on me has been a waitress and friend for over thirty years—of course, at different restaurants in our community. My wife has taught her children in school, and she is just a delightful person. Whenever I walk into the restaurant, she prepares my order. It is while I am sitting there, generally, that someone I know will stop by and say hello. Having lived in the area for over thirty-five years and served as a pastor, counselor, and chaplain at a local hospital (and in hospice for thirty-four years), chances are good that someone I know will stop by.

One day, a particular person stopped as I was writing, and this is her story. The first time we met was when her husband was lying in a hospital bed in their living room. I can still picture the room with the bed, and Jane (not her real name) was sitting in her reclining chair next to it. That recliner was her station; she even slept there. She had sat there for weeks on end, taking care of her physically declining husband. When she saw me that day in the restaurant, she and her daughter came and gave a big hug. We have a history; I was there the day her spouse went into the hospice program. I had sat in the living room and explained the program and the help we could offer in caring for her and her husband. In this particular situation, he was in very poor physical condition when we met, and he died a short time later. It was after his death that she became involved in our bereavement group. She came every month, brought friends and family members, was supportive of others in their loss, and found strength in her grief experience. She came to group for over a year. When we met in the restaurant, her first words were, "It will be thirty-five months tomorrow. since my husband died. It never goes away. You just learn to live with it differently." Each individual has his or her particular way of expressing what is happening in his or her life. My desire in presenting this information is

215

that all who are reading it will feel a freedom to express their feelings about their loss. It was without a second thought that Jane began to speak about her husband and her life. She knew that I wanted to know and that she would find acceptance.

Death and loss will come before you in a restaurant, mall, grocery store, and even when taking a walk. Grief is not an intrusion on present life but memories of the past that come and visit. The goal of grief is not to forget but to give permission not to forget, to learn how to "live with it differently." Memories come forward in today's experiences. Jane also had a question for me: "I have a friend whose spouse recently died, and she needs your help. Will you talk with her?" I remember a time when Jane felt there was no one who understood. She was a young widow. There was no one in her circle of friends who had experienced the death of a spouse. She had a very loving, supportive family and church, and some of the older widows at her church offered their support and encouragement. The church meant a lot before her husband's death and meant everything to her afterward. The people there were able to help in her transition. When you walk into a local restaurant, it may not be a chance encounter but an opportunity to remember.

Another "chance" encounter occurred not in a local restaurant but when I traveled to Jerusalem, Israel, on a tour. While walking through the area known as Gordon's Tomb (named for the person who discovered this location as a possible burial site of Jesus), I heard a voice call my name. No, it was not God; it was a person I had known in the past. Her husband and two sons had been killed years earlier, and there she was in Jerusalem, newly married to a minister. She left the group she was with to come and tell me her story. There in the setting of the empty tomb of Jesus Christ, we met again for the first time in years. The intersections of life, past and present, will continually happen. Appreciate them, embrace them, and never be threatened by them. Live expecting to discover life each day, a life in which the present and the past intersect. If we can learn to be open with grief and embrace the past as it breaks through into the present, the present will not be awkward as if something is wrong with today's life, especially when someone who represents that period of grief crosses your path.

Remember, the embrace you receive may be the embrace you needed to give. You cannot touch someone without receiving a touch. Even in a faraway country with your life on a new path, the past will come before you. Greet it and embrace it not as a threat to the present but as a gentle reminder. Life is short; value the trip because you will not pass through this moment again. Live and love each day.

Unit 90

Momentary Grief

Momentary grief occurs at the times when grief returns after a noticeable absence, such as the birthday of the deceased or an anniversary of a loved one who died twenty-five years ago. Memory is a good thing. We grieve because our loved ones are not with us; we remember because we love. Do not be frightened—grief as it was experienced earlier is not returning. You are experiencing a sorrow concerning the absence of a life that is no longer with you; you are sad that your loved one died and cannot share the day with you. This particular day has its own memory and feeling. Perhaps you are not even intentionally thinking about what day it is, but there is a sadness about the day that you just cannot put your finger on. Then, perhaps when looking at the calendar, it dawns on you: *Oh, today is the day Dad had his stroke and went to the hospital.* It can be a doctor's visit, a birthday, an anniversary of some personal significance, and so on.. These memory moments are part of life and always will be.

Unit 91

Again, Another Loss

The longer we live, the greater the chances become of other significant deaths happening in our lives. When the next significant death occurs, the past death experience will come back to us, as if we are now dealing with grief from a combination of two deaths. It is important to separate the experiences as much as possible. They will have many of the same feelings and perhaps the same emotions, but they are for two separate and distinct people. Keep them separate by attaching memories and events with each person. One man spoke of how astonished he was that his mother's death as a child and the death of his wife as an adult felt so similar. Just as our loved ones are two distinct individuals, we have two distinct relationships and separate levels of grief. My mother-in-law was a postmaster, and in her small town of Penn, each person had his or her personal mailbox that required a combination to unlock. The person distributing the mail would place the appropriate mail in the correct individual's box. Likewise, when we experience multiple deaths, we need to separate or place the emotions and events connected to each individual's life in his or her "box." Grief is not something we roll together in one lump; it calls for separating the individuals, the emotions, the relationships, and the events and keeping them with the correct people. This will help in keeping this difficult time manageable.

Unit 92

Should I Remarry?

There will come a time in our future when life will be our new normal. My mother-in-law was married for twelve years when her husband died, leaving her a young widow with a nine-year-old daughter. She never expressed interest in having another companion and never went on a date. She was happy, content, and fulfilled with her life. Other bereaved spouses have met people they fell in love with and remarried. Each person chooses what is best for his or her life. Companionship and friendship can add a special component that complements another's life. This desiring or not desiring to be with another is a personal choice. Neither of these positions should be pushed, peddled, persuaded, or encouraged so as to force a direction. We love people for who they are, how they complete our life, and how we complete them, never as replacements. If our lives are complete the way they are, then nothing else is needed. I have witnessed adult children who are married disown their surviving parent for remarrying. I have witnessed a four-year-old determine that a parent could not remarry. The decisions of life can certainly be made with input from others, but only you can determine the course for your life. You are to choose what is best for you. When one individual asked what he should do about getting married, he began to tell me what people were saying. My response was, "If you are going to do what people say, why not place an ad in the newspaper asking how many would or would not be in favor of your marriage and go with the vote?" (Obviously, this was a joke.) If you allow others to direct your life, chances are that the future you desire will not come to be. Happiness lies within your heart, and the question you need to ask is, What is it that brings happiness, contentment, and fulfillment to my life? The key here is knowing your own heart. Perhaps today there is a desire to enjoy the sunshine, to feel the breeze, to enjoy the company of friends, to take a walk, to go for a ride, or to just be who you are now that life is as it is—open, honest, and alive.

Some may be struggling and wondering, *Who am I now that I am no longer the wife of or husband of my loved one?* Some women have changed their last names back to their maiden names, looking to find that identity they willingly gave to another. For them, it was an important assertion that they were beginning again. Everyone has his or her own route. Many days are filled with decisions and questions, but at this point you have moved through some of the most difficult periods that anyone can face and have come to your new normal. You have emerged from the path in the woods. "If I marry again, will I still remember my first spouse?" you may ask. Of course you will. We love people for who they are, and they will forever be those people who occupied that time and place in our lives. We cannot remove that section of life, nor should we try. But do not keep reliving the past with another person; it may be more than the new relationship can handle. Should another person come into today's life, he or she is not there to replace anyone or to fill the empty shoes or the empty chair. This person is an individual with a new chair and wearing his or her own shoes, who is loved for the person he or she is. The feelings may be similar—maybe a few character traits are the same—but this person is a unique individual, just as you are. The same principle applies for you in that you are not a replacement in his or her life; you are loved for whom you are.

Unit 93

Replacing

In the struggles of grief, the thought of replacing the one who has died may seem like a good idea—*If I just had someone else, it would take away the pain of grief.* But replacing will not work. People are not interchangeable, as if a new part inserted into life will make life work again. We cannot superimpose a new person over a previous one and make the new one fit the mold. All this creates is more pain because at some point in the future, we will awaken and realize that the new person is not who we thought he or she was, and it will not be that person's fault. Please know that there can never be a replacement. If you try it, you will constantly be trying to correct the actions, words, and character of the replacement to fit the image of the one who has died. It is true that we are attracted to certain character traits, physical traits, and of course, the personality that best fits with our own. Each person likes certain traits in others and looks for those in people they spend a lot of time with. That is not the same as replacing. In replacing, the objective is to divert grief emotions so that we do not have to deal with them, as if a new person will stop the lonely feelings of a loved one's death. It is a sad experience for both the bereaved and the victim of this deception. I remember the sadness of a woman sitting with her dying husband. He was speaking of his love for his first wife, saying that he never told her he loved her and how much he missed her, grieving over her death. The present wife sat there and said, "In the years we have been together, I don't think he ever knew me." Each person is unique. No one can replace another, and no one can step into another's shoes. Grieving is moving through the separation of loss and from what once was; this separation prepares us for future living. Then, the desire or wish to meet another becomes a possibility. The focus has moved.

Unit 94

Hope

Hope is not conditional. Godly hope is eternal—living or dying, happy or sad, I am living in hope. Our conflict is with death, not hope. Death gives the impression that it can crush the longings of hope. Death declares hope to be lost. But the fact is that hope does not die with death. The hope addressed here is hope that cannot be diminished with conditions or trials of life for it is God-based hope. Hope is not wishful thinking. I do not profess to understand life and certainly cannot understand death or disasters. However, hope exceeds all events of life. Hope is born by the Holy Spirit and is eternal. Where hope lives, so does life. Hope is not happiness. Happiness depends on events and feelings, and hope-based life is in God and His eternal Word. Hope in Scripture speaks with certainty of events that have not yet happened, such as the hope of the resurrection of all believers. This resurrection is a certainty and as of now has not yet materialized. Hope in humankind is the desire that people will do the correct thing; this hope can seem more of a nightmare, devastated by nightly news. Some people are godlike in their love and care, and some are evil, bringing despair. Godly hope is the footing found in one another where love fits life together. The Holy Spirit forms this in our character. Every person is responsible for his or her actions. Each person will face an all-knowing God, and in that personal judgment, intentions for our decisions will be acknowledged. There is hope in our life that we are safe and hope for our loved ones that they are safe. We are in the hand of God, and nothing can drive a wedge between us—hope. We turn evil and its deeds over to God for His discerning verdict. Hope is eternal, based on God's love, His mercy, and His forgiveness. I am not alone. God is with me. I live in hope, knowing I am safe in His care. The building of hope is in Jesus Christ. He is the solid foundation of hope.

> Nay, in all these things we are more than conquerors through him that loved us. For I am persuaded, that neither death, nor life, nor angels, nor principalities, nor powers, nor things present, nor things to come, nor height, nor depth, nor any other creature, shall be able to separate us from the love of God, which is in Christ Jesus our Lord. (Romans 8:37–39 KJV)

Hope.

Unit 95

Mary, Martha, and Lazarus

The story of Mary, Martha, and Lazarus is perplexing; it is one that forces us to see beyond the immediate circumstances. These three were the closest friends of Jesus outside of the disciples. When Jesus visited Bethany, he stayed with this family. When Lazarus was sick, the two sisters knew exactly what to do. They sent for Jesus, who was not in the town. But for whatever reason, Jesus delayed his return to Bethany with the declaration to the disciples that Lazarus was dead. Some feel that Lazarus had already died by the time the news reached Jesus and that delaying a few days was not going to change anything. However, Mary and Martha were expecting Jesus to return immediately to heal Lazarus, but this did not happen. When Jesus arrived in Bethany, Martha ran to Jesus and said, "Master, if you'd been here, my brother wouldn't have died" (John 11:21 MSG). This is Martha's *why* question! Martha believed things would have, should have, and could have been different had Jesus arrived on time. In our lives, we pray and we believe that things will be different if God will just answer our prayers. Lazarus, the one "Jesus loved," was sick and dying. There was no question about this very real, loving friendship. We have all heard, perhaps since our childhood, "Jesus loves me." Human logic tells us that if He loves us and He loved Lazarus and his two sisters, whatever they requested, He would grant it. *If He loves me, He should respond to my request. That is what I would do.*

Our perspective of faith and life is limited and short-sighted. We see life in the things that touch us in the moment. We make plans for life to be extensions of what we experience in the present, acting as if our plans are divine in origin and forbidding God to change what we determine as good. Sickness and death happen to the greatest of plans, even for those who are best of friends with Jesus. Life happens. When people are sick, we pray. Our prayers are expressions of love and of what we believe to be best for living. By "faith" in God, we make these declarations. The challenge for trust, for faith, and for believing is in maintaining this level of certainty when life does not go as planned. Faith and prayer are expressed in presenting requests to God. This is our declaration of trust, believing that God will reveal Himself by altering the present state of affairs to honor the request.

What type of people would we be if we did not act upon what we believe? We pray for restoration of life, for life to continue as it was. We beg, believe, and hope that our loved ones will continue living with us. If you have ever been in a trauma center or sat in the critical care area of a hospital, you know what I am saying. Then, in times when loved ones are suffering, we pray for the suffering to cease; we pray that they will die and no longer be in pain. This is not a lack of belief. As with any request, it is an expression of love for the person and for God.

Jesus was not upset with Martha when she confronted Him about being late. Martha tells Him that if He had made it there when she sent for Him, He could have done something to help Lazarus live. After all, he was His best friend and her brother. He answered her, "You don't have to wait for the end. I am, right now, Resurrection and Life. The one who believes in me, even though he or she dies, will live. And everyone who lives believing in me does not ultimately die at all. Do you believe this?" (John 11:25–26 MSG). The challenge to Martha and to us is whether our faith is as complete in death as it is when Jesus is summoned to come quickly so that our loved one will live. Lazarus's death does not change who Jesus is: "I am, right now, Resurrection and Life." For Martha, Lazarus's death challenges what she understands Jesus to be.

As we place her statement beside our lives and beside our grief and loss, it brings Martha and us very close. Things have not changed that much in two thousand years. This is where we live, right next to Martha and to Jesus, hearing His Word and believing that we know and understand life and death. We know God can do the miraculous. We sent for Him and we prayed, and then something foreseen happened. (*If you had been here, he would not have died.*) Our loved ones die, there is no divine intervention, and our prayers appear to go unanswered. When prayers do not alter the outcomes as instructed, questions arise. We are not God, nor are we His advisors. Personal expectation, faith, and loving desire form and convey our words, thoughts, and prayers to God, seeking His intervention. The person of interest is Jesus Christ, who hears and answers prayer. He is the author and finisher of faith. He promises to never leave or abandon us, as with Martha He declares, "I am Resurrection and Life." This has not changed. We live with His promises, which are the strength of life. "Do you believe this?" The challenge for Martha was not her belief that Jesus is the miracle worker but the greater revelation that Jesus is "Resurrection and Life."

Mary, the other sister, then came out to meet Jesus, and she made the same declaration. "Mary came to where Jesus was waiting and fell at his feet, saying, 'Master, if only you had been here, my brother would not have died' (John 11:32 MSG). There is no question about the love Jesus had for Lazarus. John 11:3 (MSG) says that when the sisters sent for Jesus, the message was, "Master, the one you love so very much is sick." There is no question about the ability of Jesus to perform the miraculous, and there is no question about the faith of these two sisters and even of Lazarus. The Scripture also says of Jesus, "Now that we know what we have—Jesus, this great High Priest with ready access to God—let's not let it slip through our fingers. We don't have a priest who is out of touch with our reality." (Hebrews 4:14-15 MSG). The feelings that touch our heart touch His. This section of John's gospel contains the shortest verse in Scripture but one that also reveals Jesus's close connection to those He loves: "Now Jesus wept" (John 11:35 MSG). He is moved by the sorrow felt with death and separation. The human sorrow of loss touches the heart of God. The sadness of Mary and Martha, their questions, and their mourning—a grief that humans experience as they pass through this shadow of death— saddens the heart of God. Jesus could have dismissed the sadness with the knowledge that, in a few moments, he was going to raise Lazarus from the dead, but Jesus identified with Mary and Martha in their loss. He felt their pain. He wept with them.

The rational part of me simply declares that all of this could have been different if Jesus had arriving in Bethany in time to keep Lazarus from dying, preventing this pain and sorrow. Can there be a greater plan and a greater good in the works when Jesus does not come and heal our loved ones? Is there a greater plan when Jesus stands with us and declares, "I am Resurrection and Life"? The biblical narrative discloses that, within a few days, Jesus died on the cross. How would the sisters view the death of Jesus knowing that just a few days had passed since their brother was dead and Jesus had called him from the tomb? How would they process their belief in Jesus as He died before their eyes?

They would know firsthand that death was not what they imagined it to be, especially when Jesus declared, "I am Resurrection and Life." Jesus accompanied Mary and Martha to the tomb of Lazarus. When Jesus requested them to open the tomb, Martha objected. "Martha said, 'Master, by this time there's a stench. He's been dead four days!" (John 11:39 MSG). She was reminding Jesus how ill-mannered and disrespectful of the law it would be to open the tomb. How could she move from the crushing blow of Jesus's not coming as expected and to opening the grave of Lazarus? What was Jesus thinking? This is Jesus's challenge to Mary and Martha, and their response speaks of disbelief at such a strange request. They assert that his body has started to decay, his life is gone, the soul has departed, and Lazarus is dead.

This narrative is proof of Jesus's power over death. It is leading us to the crucifixion of Jesus and His resurrection. He is the "Resurrection and Life." Not only can He call Lazarus from the grave, He Himself will rise from the dead. These two events add authority and insight to the understanding that death cannot stop life; life is eternal, and in the resurrection, life will return to one's resurrected body.

When life leaves our bodies, mortal life changes to eternal life. Our loved ones are with Jesus in heaven, and Jesus is also with us, imparting divine hope and comfort. Remember; our faith does not cancel out our grief, and grief does not cancel out our faith. Hope and grief interlock and grow together. The two are not like oil and water, never combining no matter how much you stir. Our grief and hope are like hands clasped together, fingers interlocking with one another, perhaps with elbows on the table and our foreheads leaning into these clasped hands as we trust and receiving God's comfort.

Then there are the skeptics. "Others among them said, 'Well, if he loved him so much, why didn't he do something to keep him from dying? After all, he opened the eyes of a blind man" (John 11:37 MSG). The enemies of Jesus and the enemies of faith are individuals who find ways to be critical of previous good. Notice that in their mocking, they confirmed that Jesus had performed a miracle by healing the blind man, but they presented this miracle as a failure in comparison to not being there to heal His friend. The goal of the skeptic is engendering distrust; they do so by comparing a previous good to a present failure. The fault finders spoke what others were thinking: *If Jesus was a friend of Lazarus, couldn't He have stopped him from dying?* Mary and Martha confirmed that they felt this way. The death of Lazarus, in their minds, was not necessary. The same feelings and questions come to us when that which we believe should happen does not materialize. Faith believes its qualities to be a guarantee that if you possess a certain level of faith, that life, health, and our prayers will be answered as requested.

When a person is hanging between life and death and a doctor states, "It is up to God now," we pray for Jesus to touch and heal our loved ones to restore them to health. While we sit there in the room watching and waiting, expecting and hoping for the miraculous, it is in this place that we are like Mary and Martha, praying, "Jesus, the one you love is sick. Come quickly." When the loved one dies, we pray, "Jesus, if you had been here, our brother would not have died." Do not allow the questions or the misunderstandings of life and death to roll a stone over the entrance to your heart. The truth of Scripture brings comfort, but we grieve the death and this personal loss. This is not being selfish. This is loving someone, and when that person is no longer with us, we grieve. The comfort of the Word by the Holy Spirit comes to all who mourn. "I am Resurrection and Life"—do you believe this? Holding and hugging may be comforting as others try to help and we try to grasp what has happened, but the comfort does not stop the tears. Comfort supports us as our minds and bodies express the hurtful sorrow.

After Martha objected to Jesus's proposal to roll the stone away, Jesus looked at Martha and said, "Didn't I tell you that if you believed, you would see the glory of God?" (John 11:41–42 MSG). The sisters wanted Lazarus to be healed in a "normal miracle." They wanted him to recover from his sickness. Belief is short-sighted and limited to expectation, but what God accomplished in the sickness and death of Lazarus is greater than anyone could imagine. Our disappointment sees the failure, the unanswered prayer, and the death of a loved one. But there is an answer to each prayer, an outcome to each situation, life after death, heaven, and the resurrection of the dead. "Remove the stone" is also a call for us to remove the restrictions of being short-sighted regarding the death of our loved ones. Knowing that our loved ones are in heaven does not remove the pain of loss, the sense of failure that we perhaps did not do enough or have enough faith, or the sense that somehow God was not answering prayers that day. But we can remove the barriers that make us feel that death is a failure. See Jesus coming to your broken heart and saying, "I am, right now, Resurrection and Life" (John 11:25 MSG).

Our loved ones' bodies are in the grave. Everything of life is with God, and it is in this place of assurance that we grieve. Nothing changes the outcome of death, but we live in the light of hope, of grace, of mercy, of heaven, and of the future resurrection.

> Now, let me ask you something profound yet troubling. If you became believers because you trusted the proclamation that Christ is alive, risen from the dead, how can you let people say that there is no such thing as a resurrection? If there's no resurrection, there's no living Christ. And face it—if there's no resurrection for Christ, everything we've told you is smoke and mirrors, and everything you've staked your life on is smoke and mirrors. Not only that, but we would be guilty of telling a string of barefaced lies about God, all these affidavits we passed on to you verifying that God raised up Christ—sheer fabrications, if there's no resurrection.
>
> If corpses can't be raised, then Christ wasn't, because he was indeed dead. And if Christ weren't raised, then all you're doing is wandering about in the dark, as lost as ever. It's even worse for those who died hoping in Christ and resurrection, because they're already in their graves. If all we get out of Christ is a little inspiration for a few short years, we're a pretty sorry lot. But the truth is that Christ *has* been raised up, the first in a long legacy of those who are going to leave the cemeteries. (1 Corinthians 15:12–20 MSG)

They removed the stone. Jesus raised his eyes to heaven and prayed, "Father, I'm grateful that you have listened to me. I know you always do listen, but on account of this crowd standing here I've spoken so that they might believe that you sent me" (John 11:43–44 MSG). Jesus wanted the people standing around the tomb to know that this was not the "Jesus Show" but that He was there on a divine mission, living His life as a servant to fulfill the will of the Father.

Then Jesus said, "Lazarus, come out!" and he came out, a corpse, wrapped from head to toe, stumbling to the entrance, with a kerchief over his face. Jesus told them, "Unwrap him and let him loose." Jesus gave instructions to undo his burial wrappings, which usually consisted of a long piece of linen that enveloped the length of the body and then pieces wrapped around the body. There was much rejoicing. Lazarus was alive, back from the dead. In this moment, all was right with the world. We, like Mary, Martha, and Lazarus, have a very limited view of life; we have an incomplete outlook, and we know only what experience and understanding teach us.

The answers regarding life and death are in Jesus Christ, His birth, His Word, His life, His teaching, His death, and His resurrection. In Jesus Christ is where peace comes to our lives even when the answers to our *why* questions do not come. As we embrace the crucifixion of Christ as a willing sacrifice and move to His resurrection, all of Christ's teachings and actions come together. The things Jesus taught and the miracles He performed now take on an entirely different meaning; they confirm the words spoken by Jesus and give us insight into the love and character of God. We then, like Mary and Martha, find hope in Jesus Christ even when He does not arrive "on time," when our prayers go unanswered, and when our lives do not match our expectations. He remains our hope. Mary and Martha said, "Jesus, if you had been here, our brother would not have died," but in looking back over the events, we discover that Jesus was aware of all that was about to take place. It was all for our benefit and God's glory. It was not a mistake for Lazarus to die. Life's events do not catch Jesus unaware. He, Jesus, is Lord of life, Lord of hope, Lord of all.

After the raising of Lazarus, the officials in Jerusalem wanted to kill both Lazarus and Jesus and stop this radical movement. In a short time, they would crucify Jesus and He would rise from the dead Himself. The connection between the resurrection of Lazarus and the resurrection of Jesus—and the future resurrection of all believers—comes into view. It is not stated if Lazarus was around when the crucifixion took place or purposefully kept out of sight. Today, we would make a movie about

Lazarus and publish his views concerning life after death. But Lazarus is not the focus; Jesus is. It is His Word we take as our view of life and death. He is the one crucified for the sins of humanity. His death and burial would be the sacrifice to atone for sin, and His resurrection demonstrates the power of His life over death. The understanding of life after death does not come from the experience of Lazarus but of Jesus. The power to raise the dead is not in Lazarus; it is in Jesus Christ. He is the life that conquers death, hell, and the grave. Lazarus needed the power of life that is Christ to return to the community of his family. Jesus is life.

The supremacy of God is above any healing or rearranging of circumstances. Please know that God can and does heal and rearrange circumstances—nothing is beyond possibility—but life is about the greater picture of Christ in us and the hope of eternal life. Lazarus would physically die again at a later date. He would live his life knowing that death is not to be feared and that eternity is only a moment away. This instructs us to continue in belief and to have the courage to believe when the circumstances and the outcomes do not align with the personal desires we express in prayer. We pray and continue to believe knowing that we have eternal life through our confession of faith in Jesus Christ. Eternal life is now alive in us. I live life not to force the hand of God but to see the hand of God working everything to a divine plan. At times, that means healing and the rearranging of circumstances, and at other times, it means I find myself thinking, *Jesus, if you had been here, my brother would not have died.* No matter what may happen in life, I know that Jesus is with me. He knows what I am experiencing. He is here, and nothing can separate me from Him.

The grief of loss intertwines with the truth of Scripture, which brings hope in our sorrow with the guarantee of Scripture declaring that all who die in Christ are alive forevermore. This Word brings comfort. We grieve, but the grief and the sorrow are accompanied by the hope of eternal life in Christ. We will see our loved ones again. This understanding does not cancel our pain or our sorrow. "I am still sad when I look at the empty places in my life where my loved one lived," we may say. "But I am sustained by the knowledge that I will see them again in heaven. My life goes on. Christ strengthens me, but it is harder than I ever imagined."

Unit 96

Resurrection

The resurrection of Jesus Christ is about more than a religious holiday we call Easter. The bodily resurrection of Jesus Christ is our hope. It is the central part of the Christian faith. The resurrection speaks of life, and that life is eternal. There is a life after death. "For as in Adam all die, even so in Christ shall all be made alive" (1 Corinthians 15:22 KJV). We are eternal beings; Jesus is the resurrection and the life. Everything we believe about Jesus Christ—his teachings, his miracles, the early church, and its victory—hinges on the reality that Jesus is risen from the dead. "Jesus said unto her, I am the resurrection, and the life: he that believeth in me, though he were dead, yet shall he live: And whosoever liveth and believeth in me shall never die. Believest thou this?" (John 11:25–26 KJV). The pivotal point of human history is Jesus Christ.

I spoke once with a clergyman about the virgin birth of Jesus Christ, and I was astonished to hear him say that he did not believe in the virgin birth. He said, "It only mattered that Jesus came." He further went on to say that he did not believe in the resurrection, only that Jesus died for our sins. The apostle Paul addressed these concerns in his letter to the church at Corinth; the Scripture text was quoted earlier, from 1 Corinthians 15:12–22. Paul spoke of individuals who were trying to convince members of the Corinthian church that a resurrection was impossible. The conclusion presented by Paul is that if Jesus has not risen from the dead, then we have no hope of eternal life. Our hope is in Jesus Christ, His virgin birth, His sinless life, His sacrificial death, and His Resurrection.

Unit 97

Closing Thoughts

Being grateful is seeing the good that still exists in your life and in the family and friends around you. This is not the "birthday party" celebration but a genuine recognition of that which is good in life. Becky Lear, a friend of our family, took on the charge of reading and editing much of this book while in her own life grieving the death of her mother and caring for her father, who is in declining health. This was a journey of love, and she spoke of how grateful she was to be a part of something that will be of help to others.

I consider the hundreds of people behind the information shared in these previous units and how difficult it was to see them in their initial grief, initial brokenness, and disbelief that life could ever be good again. These lives changed, not all at once but with the time and the effort involved in allowing themselves to feel the sorrow and do something with it.

In living a life that continues to serve those who are terminally ill and their grieving families, I am well aware of how greatly life changes in just a brief moment. For many, there appears to be a confident transformation to understanding living and dying.

As I age, I see a distinction between the body growing older and the self-perception of how life and the physical body age. A soldier who fought valiantly in World War II fought, who fought through the European Theater, and fought to survive when few of those who fought with him did now in his nineties prays to die. We say it's age, but it is also a deeper understanding of life and of how the body "betrays" the life that lives within. The body fails as our place to live. As we grow older or illness ravages the body, there appears to be a definite distinction between the body and the self living in the body. Our spirits do not age; the outward appearance holds little resemblance to the inward, personal self. I know that some consider this as the rejection of aging, but what if this feeling is our inward spiritual self, the God conscience, trying to get our attention? It is that "all that is alive" self inside making itself known. Life is eternal. My life and all that is life in me will live forever, not as a sixty-six-year-old, used, failing body but as a vibrant, alive person who is always in the prime of life. Numerous times, I have been with a terminally ill person or an elderly person who declares, "My body betrayed my life" or "My body has given out but I am not finished living."

In the dying process, I have seen the struggle of wanting to live but the body failing; we identify it as "the will to live." An older woman once told me, "I feel like a rose and all my petals have been plucked." A woman in her late eighties requested that I come to the hospital and pray for this old woman in bed beside her. The "old woman" who needed prayer was at least twenty years her junior. As we age, we do not recognize or relate to the person in the mirror. How did this person get so old? Is it simply "rejecting" the image we see in the mirror? Could it be the "life breath of God," "the living soul" within letting us know that life is more than this flesh-and-blood container? Is this life inside of us declaring we are to live life not your age? Age is years; life is eternal. Eternal life is in Jesus Christ and His forgiveness.

One more thought: stop quantifying life in years. Some have a few years while others have many, but the question is, do you have life in the years? The greatest tragedy would be to live our lives and have no one grieve our absence. A child who was seven and dying of cancer said that she had lived a full life because she was loved, she loved her family, she loved God, and she knew God loved her. "I have lived a full life." She knew she was dying, she knew she was going home to be with Jesus, and she died in peace. This little seven-year-old was the most spiritual, godly person I have ever met. She died over thirty years ago, but I still have her hospital admission slip and I never will forget her. Live the life that is in your possession, and never allow what is missing to stop you from living. In Christ, life is complete. Live the life given to you. Life is a gift. Live well until you live again.

David C. McGee

Appendix

SOME ONE-LINERS TO CONSIDER:

You are the miracle someone is waiting for.

You are a miracle; you have faced obstacles of great magnitude and moved through them.

If life were over, you would not be reading this.

Your empathetic touch has a healing virtue not because you're divine but because you're human.

Touch conveys that you care.

Commitment without love is a prison without a door.

Peace without strength is only a calm before the storm

Life without breath is death.

Peace of God is peace with God.

Effort without direction is called lost.

Our greatest weakness is also our greatest strength.

What people use against you will depend on what you give them.

Hatred is pain trying to turn living into an adversary.

Fear will distort your sight, your hearing, and your will. Fear will distort the good, cripple hope, torture love, and crush the self. Fear makes your strengths out to be weaknesses and failures to be fatal. Life has no place for fear, only love.

Bringing faith and sorrow together finds healing.

Among broken hearts and shattered dreams discover a safe place for healing.

Living after death - practical considerations for an impractical time

CPSIA information can be obtained at www.ICGtesting.com
Printed in the USA
BVOW02s2225231215

430863BV00001B/1/P